Not As Prescribed

Not As Prescribed

Recognizing and Facing Alcohol and Drug Misuse in Older Adults

A Guide for Families and Caregivers

HARRY HAROUTUNIAN, MD

Foreword by Susan Ford Bales, daughter of Betty Ford

Published in collaboration with AARP® Real Possibilities

Hazelden Publishing
Center City, Minnesota 55012
hazelden.org/bookstore

Library of Congress Cataloging-in-Publication Data

Names: Haroutunian, Harry L., author.
Title: Not as prescribed : recognizing and facing alcohol and drug misuse in older adults / Harry Haroutunian, MD ; foreword by Susan Ford Bales, daughter of Betty Ford.
Description: Center City, MN : Hazelden, 2016.
Identifiers: LCCN 2015047061 (print) | LCCN 2016005186 (ebook) | ISBN 9781616496272 (paperback) | ISBN 9781616496289 (e-book)
Subjects: LCSH: Older people—Alcohol use—United States. | Older people—Drug use—United States. | Alcoholism counseling—United States. | Drug addiction—Treatment—United States. | BISAC: SELF-HELP / Substance Abuse & Addictions / General.
Classification: LCC HV5138 .H37 2016 (print) | LCC HV5138 (ebook) | DDC 362.29084/60973—dc23
LC record available at http://lccn.loc.gov/2015047061

Editor's notes
The names, details, and circumstances may have been changed to protect the privacy of those mentioned in this publication.

This publication is not intended as a substitute for the advice of health care professionals.

Limit of Liability/Disclaimer of Warranty
While AARP, the publisher, and the author have used their best efforts in preparing this book, they make no representations or warranties with respect to the accuracy or completeness of the contents of this book and specifically disclaim any implied warranties of merchantability or fitness for a particular purpose. No warranty may be created or extended by sales representatives or written sales materials. The advice and strategies contained herein may not be suitable for your situation. You should consult with a professional where appropriate. AARP, the publisher, and the author shall not be liable for any loss of profit or any other commercial damages, including but not limited to special, incidental, consequential, or other damages. The fact that an organization or website is referred to in this work as a citation and/or a potential source of further information does not mean that AARP, the publisher, and the author endorse the information the organization or website may provide or recommendations it may make. The recommendations and opinions expressed herein are those of the author and do not necessarily reflect the views of AARP. Further, readers should be aware that websites listed in this work may have changed or disappeared between when this work was written and when it is read.

20 19 18 17 16 1 2 3 4 5 6

Cover design: Theresa Jaeger Gedig; Interior design: Terri Kinne; Typesetting: Bookmobile Design & Digital Publisher Services; Developmental editor: Sid Farrar; Production editor: Heather Silsbee; and Director of AARP Books: Jodi Lipson

To my mother,
Antoinette ("Grandma Toni") Haroutunian

Contents

Foreword ix

Acknowledgments xiii

Introduction: Naming the Problem 1

Chapter 1: Older Adults in America: Driven to Drugs 9

Chapter 2: Aging, Polypharmacy, or Addiction? 21

Chapter 3: The Truth about Substance Misuse, Dementia, and Other Mental Health Disorders 41

Chapter 4: Legally Crossing the Line: Painkillers, Sedative-Hypnotics, and Marijuana 51

Chapter 5: Addiction: It's a Disease 69

Chapter 6: Finding Help: The Older Adult and Treatment 85

Chapter 7: Getting an Older Adult to Accept Help 105

Chapter 8: Every Day a Miracle 117

Chapter 9: Helping Yourself 127

Chapter 10: Staying on Track in Recovery 139

Chapter 11: Killing Pain Safely 157

Epilogue 167

Spiritual Life Must Come First 169

Resources 179

Notes 181

About the Author 187

Foreword

Just seven days shy of my mother's sixtieth birthday, the Ford family held an intervention. Betty Ford—my mother, a wife, former First Lady, breast cancer survivor, and a woman with a long list of accomplishments—was also an addict. And her addiction was overshadowing anything and everything she had ever done well in her life. And it was ruining mine.

The youngest of four children, I lived closest to our parents' home in California. Our dad—President Gerald Ford—traveled a lot, so I spent the most time with Mom during the most destructive phase of her addiction, when she stumbled, slurred her words, fell asleep midsentence, isolated herself from friends, and didn't bother to dress until late in the afternoon. Still, I was clueless about how many pills she was taking. And the doctors just kept prescribing them.

My beautiful mother, who had been a graceful dancer in her youth, a devoted and loving wife, an involved and caring parent, and a gracious hostess to world leaders visiting the White House, was now lounging around her new home in the desert, demanding that we pour stronger drinks. Betty Ford was addicted to alcohol, sedative-hypnotics, and prescription painkillers, which she had started using during her bout with breast cancer and to ease the pain of a pinched nerve in her neck. Mom and Dad grew up in the era of cocktails before dinner, and the combination of alcohol and prescription drugs was not 2 + 2 = 4.

In 1978, the year of our intervention, none of us in the family even knew what an intervention was. We were hardly familiar with the concept of addiction. And we certainly didn't fully comprehend that it was a family disease—that all of us kids and our dad were affected as well. We knew something was wrong, and we knew we didn't like how hurt and frustrated we felt by her behavior. But even with a former head of state on our team, we were clueless about how to stop Mom from what seemed like a clear path of self-destruction. She didn't listen to reason. She didn't see what we saw. As she wrote in her autobiography, *Betty: A Glad Awakening:*

> My makeup wasn't smeared, I wasn't disheveled, I behaved politely, and I never finished off a bottle, so how could I be alcoholic? And I wasn't on heroin or cocaine, the medicines I took—the sleeping pills, the pain pills, the relaxer pills, the pills to counteract the side effects of other pills—had been prescribed by doctors, so how could I be a drug addict?[1]

Almost forty years later, these words still echo through the hearts and minds of older adults who are taking mood-altering prescription medications or a toxic combination of prescribed drugs; family members are still at a loss for what to do; and doctors are still prescribing addictive medications in an effort to help their patients. *Not As Prescribed* is a valiant effort at helping concerned loved ones and caregivers of older adults understand the dynamics behind these issues, why they haven't gone away, and why they are only getting worse.

During the chaos of my mom's addiction, I was scared, I was angry, and when I saw a chance for help, I took it. I just happened to be working with a doctor who was also in recovery from alcoholism—and who conducted interventions. He agreed to help us. I told my dad that Mom needed help and that we needed to hold an intervention. He agreed. Each of us in the family participated—even my brother Jack, who had pretty much given up on Mom. We each expressed our love and support, voiced how we'd been hurt by her behavior, and asked her to get help. She agreed, reluctantly, and entered the Naval Hospital in Long Beach, California, for addiction treatment.

Before the epidemic that prescription painkiller abuse is today, before women felt safe getting help for the disease of addiction, and before the specialized treatment and recovery needs of older adults were considered relevant, Betty Ford boldly stepped into the world of treatment and recovery. Our intervention was a success—we got Mom into treatment, and she embraced recovery with a vengeance. But she didn't go with bells on her toes. In fact, there was a little kicking and screaming, at least in the beginning.

Most people in treatment are resistant, even somewhat hostile at first, but as time goes by and they open up, a change washes over them. The courage that patients acquire in their journeys is beautiful to watch, especially as they face new crises and handle them differently, with greater perspective. Sometimes the old behaviors creep back to the surface, but the new confidence will take over with the help of their Higher Power. Wonderful new relationships are waiting for people in recovery, regardless of age, and the most important of these relationships is with their Higher Power.

The words that have meant the most to me over the years are in the Serenity Prayer: "Courage to change the things I can." These words changed my world and still empower me today. And I can't forget about *hope*, which stands for How Our Pain Ends. When in the grips of my mother's addiction, I never imagined the pain could ever end. Yet it did.

Getting my mom to treatment, and then a life of recovery, wasn't easy, but it was a miracle to us. What happened afterward was a miracle for the world to see. Because we as a family went beyond our hopelessness and anger and had the courage to confront an older adult's behavior—despite the fact that she was our mother and a public figure and that we would see her tears and her wrath in response—we were able to take that important step to get her help. The most concrete miracle, as most of you know, was the founding of the Betty Ford Center, the result of Mom's strength and courage, her passing her gift of recovery forward so that other addicts and families can heal.

Not As Prescribed makes it clear that not every drug problem is an addiction problem. Sometimes, people are unwittingly taking a bad combination of drugs that cause myriad problems. Its most important message, perhaps, parallels the Ford family's experience with addiction: Every life is worth saving, regardless of age or behavior. One life in recovery can ultimately enhance the lives of thousands—including yours.

Susan Ford Bales
November 2015

Acknowledgments

Writing and publishing a book is not easy—and it's never convenient—but because I get to work and form close bonds with others on this journey with me, the process is pure joy. I'd like to especially thank Rev. Charlie Harper for his meaningful essay, "Spiritual Life Must Come First," included in the Epilogue. I know of no one who could have said it better. Linda Konner, my wise and gifted literary agent, and Karen Chernyaev, whose help with this book was immeasurable, have been my Godsends on two projects now. I know talent when I see it. I owe thanks to Sid Farrar, my editor at Hazelden, for believing in this project and for pulling from his vast pool of knowledge about addiction to make this book the best it could be. With great love, I thank my in-laws, Mike and Bobbi Resmo, and their beautiful daughter—my wife, Nicolette—for their never-ending love and support. Thank you.

INTRODUCTION

Naming the Problem

Over the years, society has adopted quite a few derogatory descriptors for alcoholics and addicts: "drunkard," "junkie," "wino," "sot." These words might stir up thoughts of slovenly, obnoxious, foul-smelling panhandlers stumbling through the streets or dazed, scab-ridden youths lounging in a coma-like state in some God-forsaken apartment or abandoned warehouse on the wrong side of town.

The stereotypical thoughts and images these words conjure up are true in some cases. But they are only a very small part of the picture. Addiction and drug misuse encompass a much larger group of people and extend far beyond dingy bars and dark alleys. The disease of addiction (yes, addiction is a diagnosable disorder, as you will read in chapter 5) is what we in the addiction recovery field call "an equal opportunity destroyer." Alcohol and drug misuse, from mild abuse to full-blown addiction, can affect anyone, regardless of race, gender, nationality, profession, income level, religious affiliation—or age. This includes older adults—moms and dads, grandparents, great-grandparents, retirees, neighbors, friends, coworkers—even those who had never experienced a problem with alcohol or other drugs during earlier life stages.

It might be hard to imagine a seventy-year-old grandfather passed out in the recliner from combining his prescription painkillers with scotch, but it's happening. And, for a host of reasons, it's happening at an alarming rate.

Addiction in older adults may be unleashed by the innocent consumption of prescription medication or the gradual increase of alcohol or marijuana intake. It may be masked by the normal symptoms of aging or the need to medicate chronic pain. In this book, we'll cover why and how our medical system and our cultural and personal belief systems are failing the older adult population like never before. And you'll learn how to help older adults deal with their substance use issues, whether it's to learn to better manage their medications, as well as any alcohol or other drug intake, or figure out whether they actually have an addiction disorder and, if so, find the right treatment program to support their recovery.

The Scope of the Problem

Drug misuse and addiction to alcohol and other drugs among older adults (which I am defining as men and women age fifty and older) is one of the fastest-growing yet most unrecognized health problems in this country. Statistics show that 17 percent of older adults misuse alcohol and prescription drugs. When we include misuse of other drugs, that number is even higher.[2] By 2020, the number of addicted older adults is expected to double to about six million.[3] Widowers over age seventy-five suffer the highest rate of alcoholism in the United States. Addiction, whether ongoing or late onset, leads to increased hospital admissions, emergency department visits, and psychiatric hospital admissions. In fact, older adults are hospitalized as often for alcohol-related problems as they are for heart attacks, one of the nation's leading killers.[4]

Notice that addiction is considered a "health problem"—not a moral failing or a sin but a problem that compromises the health and welfare of those it affects: the addict and at least five to ten family members, friends, coworkers, employers, or anyone touched by the addict's actions. And a person doesn't have to be addicted to have his or her alcohol or other drug misuse cause physical and mental health problems as well as concern among friends and loved ones.

Why Now?

Four major factors contribute to the large number of older adults now having problems with alcohol and other drugs.

First, the number of people reaching retirement age is growing by leaps and bounds. In 2011, the first of the 76 million baby boomers turned sixty-five. In what's been dubbed the "silver tsunami," every day for the next twenty years, eight thousand to ten thousand boomers in the United States will reach age sixty-five, and many will retire—with time on their hands.[5]

Second, about 50 percent of those who make up the boomer generation grew up experimenting with illegal drugs, even if only briefly.[6] When careers and raising a family took precedence, most of this generation gave up their attachment to mood-altering substances. But in retirement, or as empty nesters, a growing number of boomers are reverting to using drugs as a means of dealing with the stressors that can accompany aging—including boredom, health issues, and financial worries, as well as loss of a spouse, loss of identity, and, in some cases, loss of a certain degree of freedom. A 2011 Substance Abuse and Mental Health Services Administration study found that the rate of current illicit drug use among people in their fifties jumped by about 3.5 percent, from 2.7 percent in 2002 to 6.3 percent in 2011, indicating that the baby boomer generation is more likely than previous generations to turn to drugs as older adults.[7]

Third, since the late 1990s, when the medical community

began monitoring pain as a fifth vital sign (in addition to temperature, heartbeat, breathing rate, and blood pressure), prescription-painkiller use has experienced a dramatic rise in the United States. Worldwide, Americans take the lead, consuming about 80 percent of all prescription painkillers.[8] Painkillers such as OxyContin and Vicodin fall into a highly addictive class of drugs called opioids, which also includes heroin. Since 2002, use of prescription painkillers has doubled. The result: From 1998 to 2008 the number of people being treated for opioid abuse increased 400 percent.[9] And those who can no longer manage to get their drugs via prescription are turning to the street, where dealers have these pills readily available as well as very pure heroin—which is stronger and often cheaper than pills—creating an epidemic of frequently fatal overdoses across the country.

Fourth, older adults have been conditioned to turn to drugs for relief, whether taking a couple of ibuprofen to soothe an inflamed joint or an opioid painkiller for major back pain. According to a U.S. Census report, as many as 92 percent of U.S. adults live with at least one chronic condition; 41 percent have three or more conditions.[10] Each year, doctors write seventeen million tranquilizer prescriptions for older adults, including for benzodiazepines (think Valium, Xanax, and Ativan), the most widely misused class of drugs among that age group.[11] In 2014, Americans filled over 4 billion prescriptions at retail pharmacies alone; and adults over sixty-five fill more than twice as many prescriptions as those younger than sixty-five.[12] This is for a nation of 290 million people.

Older adults may have been comfortable using drugs in their youth, they trust their doctors to prescribe only medication that's good for them, and they trust the television commercials promoting prescription drugs. And who can blame them? Pharmaceuticals have their place in the world. They reduce suffering for millions of people every day. The problem starts when the drugs stop helping and start hurting instead. In some cases, the drug combination (whether mood-altering or not) is the culprit. In these situations, addiction is not the issue—toxic drug combinations, some of which produce dementia-like symptoms, are the problem. But when people cross the line from normal use to misuse and then dependence, addiction starts running the show. And when addiction takes over, the negative consequences start piling up and affecting loved ones like you.

Few older adults start out with a hedonistic urge to get high. Most are following doctor's orders, taking medications as prescribed. Others have been victimized by polypharmacy (taking multiple medications to help with various health issues), the result of seeing multiple doctors who don't talk to each other, coupled with a lack of patient advocacy to protect them. Others begin drinking or smoking marijuana to numb feelings of loneliness or depression that can be common in older adults for a variety of reasons. The effects of the recent decriminalization and legalization of medical marijuana in some states are, as of this writing, still largely unknown, but we will briefly explore some of the issues surrounding older adults and marijuana.

Regardless of intentions or age, the results of addiction are the same: Addiction destroys lives and families. Recovery from addiction can reverse these damages by promoting a fulfilling life that heals relationships.

Is This Book for You?

This book assumes that you have an older adult in your life whose alcohol or other drug use concerns you. If the older adult is taking four or more medications—whether mood-altering, prescribed, over-the-counter, or other—he or she may be a victim of polypharmacy, and this book is for you. If the older adult's drinking or other drug use has increased to the extent that it's affecting his or her quality of life and your relationship, read on. If anything, this book is a healthy dose of prevention. I won't tell you categorically to stop giving your loved one his or her prescribed medications or to just take away the alcohol or other drugs, nor will I advise you to make that decision. But I will take you through the concerns you're likely to have about the person's use and let you know what to look for if you suspect polypharmacy, misuse, or addiction. This book will generally increase your awareness of the issues older adults are facing today around substance use, and offer some steps you can take to ensure that your loved one does not experience, or stops experiencing, adverse symptoms because of toxic drug combinations.

If the ripple effect of misuse or addiction has reached you, this book can help you understand what's going on and what you can (and can't) do about it. Addiction has a knack for confusing the hearts and minds of loved ones, leaving you unsure and angry. As a medical doctor certified in addiction medicine, a physician director at the Betty Ford Center, an older adult, and a recovering addict, I know. I see addicted patients and their loved ones every day. Many of these patients wind up at the Betty Ford Center not by design but by complete and utter accident. Many of them were following doctor's orders, taking proper doses of prescribed medications, and being "good" patients. Suddenly, and often after only a short time, they found themselves needing more and more of a prescription painkiller or antianxiety drug.

In this book, you'll learn the tools you need to correctly identify and swiftly address drug misuse and addiction in an older adult—whether a parent, grandparent, patient, coworker, neighbor, or friend, and regardless of whether he or she is misusing alcohol, marijuana, painkillers, heroin, or other drugs. I'll show you how to take your loved one from what might be his or her lowest point in life and turn it into what potentially could be the best time of life. I will take the confusion out of harmful drug combinations, teach you how to safeguard against painkiller dependence, guide you through the addiction treatment process for older adults should that be necessary, and show you what recovery and life free of harmful drug combinations can bring.

Every addict has a unique story. At the same time, every story has common denominators with other stories of misuse and addiction in older adults. We'll cover some of those denominators and give you, a loved one or other caregiver, solid, trustworthy information that will help you take the next right action when it comes to helping the older adult in your life. Facts and fresh perspectives will move you from chaos to clarity so that, in your heart and mind, you will know what to do—and, regardless of the outcome, you will know that you have done your best to help your loved one.

■

CHAPTER 1

Older Adults in America: Driven to Drugs

You're reading this book because you have questions about the alcohol or other drug use of an older adult in your life. You might be concerned that Mom's sixteen prescribed medications are making her confused, that Dad's one martini every night is interacting with his heart medications, or that Grandma's dementia might be related to drug use. Your concern is normal and warranted. You might live hundreds of miles away and can only go by what your loved one tells you about her condition over the phone. Even if you live next door or in the same house, how can you be 100 percent certain that your loved one's behavior is only a sign of aging rather than a sign of substance misuse?

When I worked as a family practitioner, a sizeable percentage of my practice was composed of older adults. I treated several families with five generations: the great-great-grandmother, the great-grandmother, the grandmother, the parents, and the children, all under my care. I was truly blessed. From these and other families, I heard many questions about their older loved ones. And today at the Betty Ford Center, where we treat people for substance use disorders, I address many of the same questions and concerns: Has there been a behavioral change in the loved one, as well as a physical change? Is there a question of mental competency? Is Mom addicted, or is this dementia? One doctor doesn't seem to talk to the next. How can I possibly figure out all of these medications? She keeps all of her pills in one bottle, and I have no idea what they are. She has a glass or two of wine or sherry in the evening, and sometimes you can't wake her up. Sometimes she's so confused I'm surprised she finds her way around the house. What she says just doesn't make any sense.

I hear the same questions and concerns from families at the Betty Ford Center that I heard from the different generations in my family practice. These are the kinds of worries that plague families: I don't know what to do. We've been trying to care for my mother (or my father, my uncle, or my aunt), and we just don't know what to do anymore. No one seems to be able to help. There is a huge shift in Dad's behavior, and I'm afraid to leave the kids with him.

And then I have questions myself: Are we as physicians creating bodies and minds that are imprisoning our patients? Are the chemicals we prescribe or the legal chemicals that patients can purchase capable of wrapping up the mind, the heart, and the soul of patients so tightly that they are completely withdrawn from the real world? And if that is the case, how do we deal with it? How do we help families save these wonderful citizens who have given us so much and now seem so desperately lost in these later stages of life?

We can't just throw them away. I know that we can save them. It requires patience, it requires tolerance, and it requires an investigative perseverance worthy of Sherlock Holmes. But we can make a difference in their lives, and this book is all about hope and revitalization.

To revitalize is to bring life back into someone who has been lost. Let's walk this journey together, in the pages that follow, to help revitalize you and your loved one, who may possibly be caught up, even unwittingly, in the disease of addiction.

It's never too late. Compared to their younger counterparts, older adults have a greater chance of recovering from drug misuse. Older adults who go through addiction treatment have some of the best success rates for staying in long-term recovery. Leading your older loved one to a clean and sober life, and helping him or her establish a healthy relationship with necessary prescription drugs, regardless of age, is worth your time and one of the greatest gifts you will ever give.

In the introduction, I established that drug use is prolific among older adults. But certainly not every older adult has an issue with the medications he or she takes on a daily basis. Let's look at the wide expanse of possibilities and see where your loved one might fall on the continuum.

The Continuum: From Awareness to Severe Addiction

A lot of terms get bandied about when it comes to addiction. There's substance abuse, addiction, dependence, problem drinking, drug misuse. I'm sure you can think of more. But what does each term mean, and what's the difference between abuse and dependence, misuse and addiction, or any other term? How practitioners describe drug use changes in part when the American Psychiatric Association publishes an updated version of its *Diagnostic and Statistical Manual of Mental Disorders*, known in the mental health field as the *DSM*. The *DSM* is a bible of sorts for mental health practitioners. It categorizes, codes, and defines all known mental health disorders to help clinicians make a correct diagnosis. It also ensures that the diagnosis is standard across all practices, from the doctor who's working independently in the mountains of Vermont to a psychiatrist working in a large hospital setting in a megalopolis such as Los Angeles. When the *DSM*'s definition of a disorder changes, so too can the terminology.

DSM-5, the version in print at the time of this writing, uses the term *substance use disorder* and breaks it down into mild, moderate, and severe. A person who's mildly misusing substances might be drinking two or three glasses of wine every evening and getting anxious around dinnertime, when her body begins craving alcohol. A person considered to have a severe substance use disorder might wake up in the morning plotting how to get more of a drug and may have lost a job or home or committed a crime. Typically, the more advanced the substance abuse, the more severe the consequences. But, again, I emphasize that everyone is unique. The point is that a person doesn't need to be addicted to have substance misuse adversely affect her life, and a person can still be addicted without hitting "rock bottom" or having her life in shambles. Substance misuse happens on a continuum with addiction at the far end, and addiction looks different at different stages.

I'm not asking you to diagnose anyone (and I certainly can't diagnose your loved one or patient through this book), so for our purposes I simply need you to understand that this book covers a wide continuum. Regardless of whether I'm using the term *use*, *misuse*, *addiction*, *alcoholism* (addiction to alcohol), or *substance abuse*, understand that I am still speaking to you about the older adult you care about—even if his or her relationship with mood-altering substances turns out not to be problematic.

I emphasize this point because I understand that you are reading this book for helpful information, not to be told your dad is an addict when he's not. In short, this book does not assume that an older adult is an addict. This book is about awareness. If you take away anything from this book, I hope it is that the scope of the problem is wide and the continuum of substance use leaves a lot of room for interpretation. Once you understand that, you can determine your next best steps, if any, based on your unique situation.

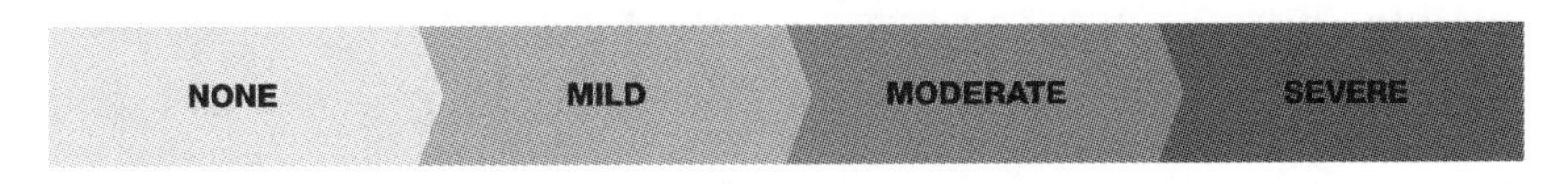

From Their Perspective: "Better Living through Chemistry"

When I talk about older adults, I am not just talking about boomers. The range that I'm using of people age fifty and older includes three to four generations: the G.I. generation (born 1901–1924), silent generation (born 1925–1945), baby boomer generation (born 1946–1964), and generation X, or what some call the thirteenth generation (born 1965–1984), because they identify as the thirteenth generation since the founding of the United States. Growing up, each of these generations was inundated with societal messages regarding how to behave, what constitutes shameful behavior, and how to view drugs, alcoholism, and other addictions. All of this and much, much more forms how a generation, in general, views itself in relation to mood-altering drugs, especially to addiction, and why someone might not want to eagerly run up to an AA podium and proudly declare that he is an alcoholic.

What follows simply scratches the surface of generational beliefs and the cultural mind-set around drug use—including prescription drugs—and addiction in the United States. But I hope it will give you some insight into some of your loved one's behaviors, such as having that morning martini in isolation, refusing to go to the doctor when you've suggested he may need help cutting back on his pain medication, or falling asleep behind the wheel after smoking marijuana.

The stigma associated with being an addict runs high in our society, especially among those born before World War II. This generation grew up associating alcoholism with "town drunks" and opioid addiction with low-life criminals, not with drug and alcohol prevention programs and treatment centers that address patients with dignity and respect. Most people from this era who suffer from alcohol or drug addiction do not see themselves as having fallen that low. If they suspect that they are an alcoholic or addict, admitting it would be too shameful. Instead, they "pull themselves up by their bootstraps" and deal with it themselves, as they have been taught to deal with all of life's problems. But they and their families soon discover that addiction is not like other life problems. It's a disease that invades the body and life not only of the addicted but also of loved ones and caregivers.

Yet for most older adults who were born in the 1920s and after, turning to addictive prescription drugs for pain relief is fairly natural. They've been conditioned to do so. The 1920s and 1930s saw the first major growth in pharmaceuticals, as companies introduced pills, sprays, and injections for nasal congestion, asthma, diabetes (insulin), and bacterial infections (penicillin). The post–World War II era brought about an explosion of new medications to help with everything from anxiety to menopause. A DuPont advertisement from the 1940s encouraged "better living through chemistry." These were modern, industrialized times when humankind exuded a sense of control over nature, including the diseases it brought. Medicine, many people began to believe, would soon cure all that ailed us.

At the time of the writing of this book, the youngest of the G.I. generation are in their early nineties. You might wonder why I include them. Even if they are addicted, why not let them live out the rest of their lives as they choose? Remember that addiction is an equal opportunity destroyer and has a ripple effect. Leaving Grandma stoned and numb in a chair might seem to make the caregiver's role easier, but Grandma is not having fun—and the debilitating effects of substance misuse actually make caregiving more difficult in the long run. If you believe life is worth living, it's crucial to make the most of however many years remain. After all, none of us knows when our time is up.

Besides, it's not unheard of for people in their nineties who have developed an addiction disorder to find recovery. My good friend Michael Walsh, president and CEO of the National Association of Addiction Providers, shared that the oldest woman he has ever intervened on was ninety-one years old: "She was drinking hard liquor every afternoon with the maintenance man at her apartment building. She got into recovery, and her world got a lot bigger. She was traveling to Europe, spending time with grandchildren. She looked twenty years younger. She made me a believer. It's never too late."[13]

The silent generation, along with the baby boomers, form the largest older adult population. But their "peer personalities" and collective mind-sets are different enough that, even in treatment, we often separate them (usually ages forty-six to sixty-four and ages sixty-five and older). While people in the silent generation are more reluctant to identify as addicts, boomers who have an addiction disorder tend to feel less stigma. Even if they didn't do drugs in their youth, boomers grew up in the love, sex, drugs, and peace culture and, in subsequent years, were more accepting of the growing number of people, including celebrities, publically identifying their addiction as a disease and seeking treatment.

In the 1960s, drugs were likely to be used to make a cultural statement. In the early 1960s, LSD was still a legal substance, and Harvard psychologist Timothy Leary, who believed the drug could be used to help treat psychiatric issues as well as "raise consciousness," advised people to "turn on, tune in, and drop out." Many in the boomer generation soaked up this counterculture mentality, which included using an assortment of illegal drugs—marijuana, heroin, PCP, amphetamines, and LSD, which had become illegal in most states beginning in the mid-sixties. The boomers couldn't have predicted that marijuana would eventually become legal in several states, in most for medical purposes only but, in a growing number, for recreational use as well. There's still a lot of controversy about this issue, with some experts believing that because marijuana is an addictive drug, we need to proceed cautiously in having it so readily available, especially for young people whose still-developing brains can be seriously impaired by overuse.

During a heyday in the pharmaceutical industry beginning in the 1950s, boomers and their parents had been exposed to barbiturates and amphetamines, which doctors freely prescribed as the cure-all for everything from dieting to emotional distress. The 1960s was the decade of "the Pill," giving women sexual freedom without the fear of pregnancy for the first time in history. Valium and Librium calmed the nerves of anxious housewives and overworked businessmen. Lifesaving drugs such as high blood pressure and other heart medications also came into being. Americans were demanding better health care, pharmaceutical companies were producing a plethora of drugs to resolve what ailed folks, and the "mad men" of advertising were getting the word out.

Whether people took legal drugs, illegal drugs, or nothing at all, they were part of a collective consciousness that was screaming out of both sides of its mouth: Legal drugs could cure all and make you happier; if you were part of the counterculture, illegal drugs could do the same, while the conservative establishment saw them as evil itself, robbing young people of success and sanity. Like it or not, legal drugs were part of American culture, and illegal drugs were part of the counterculture. No matter which side of the fence you sat on, you were exposed to the normalization of drug use. And when the time came for you to need something for pain, anxiety, or a disease, the promise of a longer life lived in better health or ridding yourself of pain or psychological discomfort simply by popping a pill was too good to pass up. You followed the doctor's orders.

If patterns of people when they're young predict their behaviors as older adults, the youngest of the baby boomers might pose the greatest problem when it comes to addiction. People born from 1961 to 1964 are now in their early to mid-fifties. Their worldview and experiences differ remarkably from generation X, and their history of alcohol, drug abuse, and violent crime stands out.

Boomers born in the early sixties were young witnesses to the conflict created by the social revolution of the sixties. Unlike many older boomers, they didn't participate in sit-ins or protests but watched them on television at a very tender age. They also saw or felt the impact of urban rioting, intense political debates over race and war, Watergate, and an unprecedented leap in divorce rates. They were the children of the rugged and hearty G.I. and silent generations, who grew up during the Great Depression and at least one world war. Their parents likely had strong opinions about what was going on. Like any cohort group that falls at the very beginning or the tail end of a generation, they are caught between two generations. For our purposes, what stands out among this cohort group is their history of drug and alcohol abuse. Of all the children born in the post-WWII period, those born from

1961 to 1964 have the highest rates of high school drinking and drug use, and driving under the influence.[14]

Common Ground among Generations

Regardless of how old we are or what generation we are a member of, all of us share common ground when it comes to alcohol or other drug misuse and addiction. We can all feel stigma, shame, and weakness of character to varying degrees at the implication that we can't control our use. We can all have some of the same thoughts: If I'm an addict, what does that mean? Is it a disease or a moral failure? How am I affecting my loved ones? Will I die a lonely, painful death in a dark place? Is my defensiveness and anger about my situation evident to others? Have I done this to myself? Have I been minimizing how alcohol and drugs affect me? How long can I disregard the evidence presented by my loved ones? How else do I explain my behavior and negative consequences? Why can't I just pick myself up by my bootstraps? Will my loved ones lose respect for me if I'm an addict and see me as a failure? Am I being punished? Will I go to hell?

Is It Age, or Is It Addiction?

Discovering, addressing, and treating drug misuse in people from the G.I., silent, and boomer generations in particular poses some unique problems. In many cases, older adults do not believe that alcohol or other drugs are the source of their problems. It's particularly difficult for older adults, their families, and even health care workers to clearly distinguish between the signs of aging and the signs of addiction, many of which overlap. Slurred speech, stumbling, and forgetfulness, for instance, can look like typical signs of aging; side effects of prescription drugs or combinations of drugs; misuse of alcohol, prescription, or other mood-altering drugs; or all of the above.

In the next chapter, I'll talk about how to distinguish between the signs and symptoms of aging, the signs and symptoms of polypharmacy (using multiple prescription drugs at the same time), and alcohol and other drug misuse, including addiction.

■

CHAPTER 2

Aging, Polypharmacy, or Addiction?

Betty is a mother of five, grandmother of eleven, and a widow. At age seventy-eight, Betty developed excruciating pain in her neck that radiated down her arm and into her upper back. She sought numerous consultations and orthopedic and neurosurgical evaluations, and underwent several MRIs before being diagnosed with degenerative disc disease and nerve impingement syndrome, or spinal stenosis.

Initially, over-the-counter painkillers were sufficient to ease her pain, but as it heightened she graduated to the more potent opioid painkillers. Betty was seeing not only her primary care physician but also a neurosurgeon and an orthopedic surgeon, one of whom had referred her to a pain specialist and all of whom were providing her with medications for her pain. Betty had bottles of MS Contin. She had OxyContin, she had Percocet, and in one attempt to put her on less addictive medications, she was given a prescription for tramadol, a "narcotic-like" pain reliever. Also, for her nerve pain she was using amitriptyline, an older tricyclic antidepressant used to treat neurologically based pain and known for its severe side effects, including dizziness, dry mouth, constipation, and weight gain. To top it off, she was placed on Tegretol and Neurontin, antiseizure medications for her neuropathic pain.

Everyone seemed to be trying desperately to relieve this poor woman's discomfort and to avoid the inevitable surgery that would release her neck impingement. But that was not the least of her medical problems. She was also treated for benign positional vertigo (the feeling that everything is spinning when your head is in certain positions) with meclizine. In addition, she was being treated for a spastic colon, or irritable bowel syndrome, with Levsin, and she was in the habit of trying to get a good night's sleep at times with Tylenol PM or Benadryl, and at times with Ambien or Lunesta.

The side effects of each drug alone are lengthy, but when combined, these drugs are capable of producing a powerful offspring of effects far too numerous to list. Suffice it to say that medications such as Benadryl and the antispasmodic used for her irritable bowel syndrome have side effects in older adults that are quite significant, not the least of which is profound memory loss.

So it was not uncommon for one of her kids to visit Betty, who had chosen to live alone, and come back reporting that "Mom is losing it, Mom needs assisted living, what are we going to do?" Her speech was slurred, she left the iron on the ironing board and burned a big scorch mark in a dish towel, she left the stove on and a pot was boiling over. Her door was unlocked. She wasn't dressed at two o'clock in the afternoon, she missed her doctor's appointment, and she lost her car keys. And well-intentioned friends visiting Betty said they were afraid she was going to burn her apartment building down.

Betty's story is not uncommon. Does this story sound familiar?

■

Linda and John have similar stories. Linda's mom's neighbor in Florida calls up Linda in New York to tell her that her seventy-five-year-old mom fell for the second time this month. She's okay, but the neighbor is beginning to worry that Mom has been slurring her words and acting unusual lately, and that perhaps she is in the early stages of dementia.

John's eighty-year-old dad, who usually awaits John's call every night at 8:00 p.m., has stopped answering the phone on some nights. He tells John that he falls asleep in his chair by the phone.

These stories of aging adults are just a few of millions. What do these behaviors tell us?

More often than not, they are normal signs and symptoms of aging. In many cases, however, drugs—whether alcohol, prescription drugs, marijuana, or a combination—play a role. In this chapter, I'm going to help you distinguish among the three most common reasons an older adult may start acting differently: normal aging, polypharmacy, and misuse or addiction.

Normal Aging

Aging is a normal process that's generally quiet and slow, involving subtle changes over time. It's neither good nor bad; it just is. It begins the day we are born. By about age thirty, most of us have reached our physical peak. Cells begin to regenerate more slowly. But we don't necessarily notice this right away. Over the years, depending on our genetics; our environment; and our beliefs, behaviors, and attitudes—as well as how well we take care of ourselves—we might start to see gray hairs, an expanding waistline, and wrinkles, and to feel general aches and pains, increasing fatigue, and a slowing of our metabolism. The extent and timing of these events vary from person to person and even culture to culture. Some forgetfulness and other diminishment of cognitive abilities, as well as loss of balance, hearing, and eyesight, are also common. However, sudden or dramatic changes in these abilities or behaviors are red flags that something isn't normal and possibly requires medical attention. The same goes for the sudden onset of pain that is more severe than the normal aches and pains that go with aging. Some of the signs and symptoms of normal aging can be prevented or even reversed if we take good care of ourselves by eating healthy foods, exercising, and taking measures to reduce and address chronic stress.

Polypharmacy

Drugs can be powerful agents for healing. But when taken in excess or in the wrong combination, they can be problematic and even deadly. As already noted, polypharmacy is the taking of multiple medications for coexisting conditions, such as diabetes, high blood pressure, and chronic pain. In the United States, about half of adults over age sixty-five take five or more medications per week. About 12 percent of those sixty-five and older take ten or more medications per week, including over-the-counter (OTC) drugs such as aspirin, ibuprofen, and acetaminophen, and supplements such as vitamins, minerals, and herbs.[15] When combined, many drugs and supplements can create adverse reactions, leading to balance problems that cause falls, confusion, and urinary incontinence. To make matters worse, in many instances, when the patient goes to the doctor complaining of something like loss of balance, the doctor prescribes yet another drug to treat the new but (unbeknownst to the doctor) drug-induced and reversible symptom, a common phenomenon referred to as a "prescribing cascade."

Doctors aren't always to blame. They are trained to treat the symptom. They work, for the most part, independently in a health care system that is not necessarily set up to monitor what other doctors at other facilities are doing for the same patient. And the older we get, the more likely we are seeing multiple specialists. For irritable bowel syndrome, we see our gastroenterologist. For our rheumatoid arthritis or lupus, we see the rheumatologist. For hypertension and cardiovascular heart disease, we visit the cardiologist. For vertigo, we see the neurologist. For leukemia, we see an oncologist. For diabetes, we visit the endocrinologist and for our rotary cuff injury, the orthopedist. You get the picture. Older adults, especially, trust that their health care providers know what's going on and that they wouldn't possibly prescribe something harmful. And they wouldn't—at least not intentionally.

Mom slurring her words might not be because she's abusing her painkillers but because she's taking (under doctors' orders) a number of prescription drugs that, when combined, interfere with her speech. Linda's mom, described at the beginning of this chapter, was taking seventeen different prescription drugs for arthritis, cardiovascular disease, and gastrointestinal complaints. The combination of a beta-blocker and an antispasmodic, when added to the Klonopin she was taking to calm her nerves, caused her to lose her balance and slur her words, giving the false impression that she was drunk or developing dementia.

Most of the older adults I see at the Betty Ford Center come in taking five to twenty different legally prescribed drugs. Through no fault of their own, they have become victims of polypharmacy. It's not unusual to have a nurse call me in to see what medications a patient has brought in. When I enter the room, I may see eight bottles of supplements, all of which have potential side effects. And I may also see twelve or fifteen prescription bottles, all from different physicians, all of whom failed to communicate with one another or to take the medication audit necessary to determine what a patient is actually putting into his body every day and then calculate how the medications may interact.

And we haven't even mentioned alcohol—also a drug and one that adversely interacts with almost all other drugs, including antibiotics, antidepressants, anticoagulants, antihistamines, and antidiabetic and antiseizure medications, as well as narcotic and nonnarcotic pain relievers and tranquilizers. Alcohol-medication interactions can be serious, as one drug infringes on the body's metabolization of another, rendering it less effective and causing symptoms such as nausea, vomiting, headache, convulsions, hemorrhages, liver damage, a rise in blood pressure, or loss of consciousness, as well as injury and even death from overdose. In the older adult, whose metabolism has slowed, these interactions can be even more serious, as the drugs stay in the body longer.

As mentioned, Americans filled over 4 billion prescriptions in 2014. An estimated 25 percent of emergency department visits are related to bad alcohol-medication interactions.[16] Most of us don't think twice about taking two aspirins and going out for dinner and drinks. In the older adult, that simple combination can, over time, cause gastric bleeding, increase the inebriating effect of the alcohol, and lead to falls and injuries.

Polypharmacy in and of itself is a major issue among the elderly, with as many as 35 percent of older adults experiencing an adverse effect and 29 percent requiring hospitalization.[17] Polypharmacy can also lead to addiction.

Addiction

Substance misuse, including its most severe form, addiction, comes in all shapes and sizes. It depends on genetics, environment, brain chemistry, personality, and the addictive nature of the hundreds of different mood-altering substances available. Some people are drinking alcoholically from the first drink, while others can misuse alcohol for years and then decide at some point to stop or are able to cut their intake and become "social" drinkers. Taking an opioid painkiller as prescribed for more than two to four weeks for some people has no negative effect, and for others it is enough to make them want to come back for more. Most people who smoked marijuana regularly in the 1960s and 1970s simply stopped once they got responsible jobs and had families, while some became habitual smokers and became addicted.

When we decide to take four instead of the prescribed two

pills once, we're pushing the limit; repeating that behavior daily or weekly is misuse. This can lead us to develop a tolerance for the drug so that we need more and more each time we take it in order to feel as we did when we first took the prescribed two pills. We're starting to depend on it not only physically but also emotionally. We start to fear that, without it, we will suffer. And, in all likelihood, we *will* suffer. Our brains have already started to adapt to the medication, abating its effectiveness.

By the same token, asking a neighbor if we could have one of his leftover painkillers to ease stomach cramps seems innocent enough, but it's also pushing the limit—the medication was not prescribed to ease our stomach cramps. In fact, it wasn't even prescribed to us. Misusing mood-altering substances can start out innocently enough—it's just an attempt to feel better. But if the behavior continues, in some people, addiction can take over.

Addiction is when a mood-altering substance becomes the priority in our lives: We become preoccupied with the thought of getting our next drink or fix. We have lost the ability to decide if we're going to drink or use, or how much. We cross the line from enjoying a casual drink to *needing* a drink. Our continued use reprograms and highjacks our brains by replacing the brain's normal production of dopamine, one of the body's "feel-good" chemicals. The brain registers an overflow of dopamine every time we drink or pop a pill, and so it stops producing the natural chemical that once made us feel pretty good without an outside mood-altering substance. When we stop drinking or taking our drug, our bodies are void of dopamine and so we crave our drug and a fresh new supply of the feel-good chemical. Although the body can heal and begin producing dopamine again on its own, our cravings are too strong to wait, and we don't give it a chance.

John's dad, mentioned in the beginning of this chapter, had

always been a good provider and a solid, stable, and trustworthy parent. He had been grieving the recent loss of his wife of forty-five years. Sitting alone watching television every evening, he got in the habit of pouring a scotch or two after the evening news, a program he used to watch with his wife every night. Within a few months, his use escalated to three and then four drinks, which would cause him to fall asleep in his chair before his son called. John thought his dad's fatigue was due to age, which could be entirely possible. But in this case, alcohol was the problem, and John's dad had crossed the line from social use to misuse. At first, he used scotch to numb his emotional pain. Eventually, he needed it to feel alive.

Knowing the Difference

So how do we tell the difference? How do we know whether our loved one is displaying normal signs of aging, is a victim of polypharmacy, or has inadvertently become addicted to alcohol, benzodiazepines, painkillers, or another drug of choice?

Many of the signs and symptoms of aging overlap with those of polypharmacy and addiction, which can make it difficult to distinguish between the conditions. To make matters worse, the signs and symptoms aren't always exclusive. Doctors, for instance, might have already established that Mom suffers from loss of balance due to aging. But how will you know whether the three falls this month were due to this condition or due to her being intoxicated? There are some telltale differences and clues.

To know what your loved one might be experiencing, you'll need an overview of some of the overlapping signs and symptoms. You'll also want to know what addiction is and isn't. You might be all too familiar with addiction—maybe an older adult in your life has been in treatment before, maybe you witnessed an uncle's transformation after he got clean and sober, or maybe you are in recovery yourself. Or you may be encountering the disease for the first time.

Later in this book, we will get into a full-blown discussion of the disease of addiction and what it means to be in recovery. For now, to help you understand what condition you're dealing with—normal aging, polypharmacy, or addiction—let's compare some signs and symptoms common to each condition and use an example or two to see how they are similar and where they differ. These examples are not specific to any particular older adult age group: A fifty-year-old might show the sign differently than an eighty-year-old. The following chart is only to illustrate how the cause of each condition can vary. As you will see, the cause is not always cut-and-dried, but knowing the how and why of a loved one's behavior is significant.

Keep in mind the statistics: about 17 percent of older adults age sixty and older are misusing alcohol or other drugs. Although it's a remarkably high percentage, it means that about 83 percent are not affected by misuse. The odds are that your loved one isn't misusing alcohol or other drugs. But recall that 50 percent of adults age sixty-five and older take at least five medications. The odds are good that an older adult in your life might be a victim of polypharmacy and, if a mood-altering medication is in the mix, could someday accidently cross the line into addiction. Understanding the difference between the signs and symptoms of aging versus those of polypharmacy and addiction can help you with prevention efforts as well.

Signs and Symptoms: Distinguishing among Aging, Polypharmacy, and Addiction

Sign/Symptom	Aging	Polypharmacy	Addiction
Neglecting responsibilities	Too tired or depressed to maintain home	Too high to realize	Alcohol/drug use is more important
Engaging in dangerous activities	Driving to keep independence	Driving under the influence (DUI)	DUI
Getting into legal trouble	Traffic violation or serious driving offense while clean and sober	Disorderly conduct due to confusion or paranoia	DUI
Problems in relationships	Isolating to grieve the loss of a spouse	Isolating because drugs are affecting cognition and awareness	Isolating to hide drinking or drug use
Forgetfulness	Onset of dementia	Bad drug combination	Too much of a drug
Changes in sleep patterns	Becomes a light sleeper	Sleeps excessively or very little	Trouble falling asleep
Abandons once-joyful activities	Lacks energy or no longer interested	Medications cause fatigue	More interested in using drug of choice
Tremors, slurred speech, impaired coordination	Neurological condition	Bad drug combination	Drunk or high
Deterioration of physical appearance	Dementia	Bad drug combination	Indifference

Knowing as much as possible about aging, polypharmacy, addiction, and your loved one's behaviors is the best first step. It helps you recognize the problem. But it only takes you so far. Your attitude is the mind-set that will take you where you need to go or stop you dead in your tracks. To be able to help Dad with his alcoholism, you have to believe that the drinking is actually a problem at his stage of life. You have to understand how his drinking is harming, not serving, him and every other life he touches.

We've already established that we live in a nation that predominantly accepts the use of legal drugs, such as alcohol, prescription drugs, and increasingly, marijuana. Let's look at some common beliefs about aging and addiction.

First Reactions: Ageism and Complacency

Typically, over time, loved ones and caregivers begin to register thoughts such as the following, based on what they know about their older adult:

- Something has changed for the worse.
- My mom is losing her mental or physical faculties due to age.
- The prescription narcotics are making my grandmother act goofy.
- Let Dad get drunk/high and enjoy what little time he has left.
- Our family needs to accept and adjust to these expected changes.

Where do you stand? If anyone who's involved in the decision-making process about Dad's welfare believes wholeheartedly that Dad should drink himself to death because he's got nothing else in life, it's time to take a close, hard look at the beliefs around aging.

Why Bother?

Ageism, defined by *Merriam-Webster's* as the "prejudice or discrimination against a particular age-group and especially against the elderly," is a prevalent cultural attitude in the United States.

Many people grow up assuming that grandmas and grandpas walk slowly, lose their thought process all the time, and don't contribute much anymore. This is our cultural heritage. Most older adults would call those judgments unfair. I know I would. So would the younger generations in cultures that revere older adults for their wisdom. Most older adults also internalize these messages so that they become part of their belief system. They start expecting their health and abilities to go south as they age. After all, today's older adults were likely guilty of ageism during their youth.

If we proclaim that Dad should live out his final days drunk or high, we're guilty of ageism. We're implying that older adults do not add value. These types of thoughts are worth looking at in a new light. After all, most of us will reach older adulthood and could face the same type of disrespect ourselves.

If we equate an older adult's addictive drinking and drugging with one of life's last hurrahs, we're shortchanging everyone involved, including ourselves. We're saying it's better to escape than it is to live. We're allowing the older adult to be more susceptible to death or serious injury. We're perhaps robbing loved ones, including grandchildren and ourselves, of quality time. We're missing an opportunity to help. We're choosing convenience over right action. And we're making a major statement, one we perhaps aren't even consciously aware of, about how we feel about what it means to be an older adult: In effect, we're saying that older adults don't add value to the world and no longer grow as individuals or have purpose.

Family members are not the only decision makers who can get caught up in ageist beliefs. Health care providers are capable of doing the same. According to a Substance Abuse and Mental Health Services Administration report on substance abuse and older adults, "Ageism is reflected in some providers' belief that older adults' quality of life will remain poor even if they are successfully treated for their substance abuse. Such lowered expectations may also be compounded by 'therapeutic nihilism': Older substance abusers may be deemed not worthy of the effort involved in treating or changing behavior because 'they are likely to die soon anyway.'"[18]

It Is What It Is

Complacency is another common reaction to changes in an older adult's behavior. Most of us, in fact, confuse complacency with acceptance. If you or others accept the changes as expected, it could be helpful to consider the difference between aging and getting old. Chronological aging is expected—twelve months pass, and we are another year older. Getting old is a mind-set. Biologically, Mom might be eighty years old with the spine of a sixty-year-old and the heart of a forty-year-old. When we expect that Mom is acting confused just because she's eighty, we don't bother to consider other issues such as polypharmacy. We, and Mom, lose out.

Once we examine our beliefs about older adults' alcohol and other drug misuse, we're no longer wavering. Any indecision we had about how or whether to intervene disappears, and suddenly and simply, we know we must do something to help.

Common beliefs about older adults and alcohol and other drug misuse, including addiction, are:

- It's the only pleasure left at this age.
- He worked hard all his life; let him enjoy himself.
- It's her money.
- She's in too much pain to abstain from painkillers.
- Happy hour is the only social activity she has left.
- He has nothing else to do.

- Who is he harming?
- Since Mom passed, it helps him with the loneliness.
- It's a disease. There's nothing you can do.
- He needs to reach rock bottom.
- The family can't afford treatment.
- He's too confused to be in treatment.
- She needs to tend to her medical problems first.
- You can't force anyone into treatment.
- He was in treatment twenty years ago. It didn't work.

But people who've addressed their misuse, including pursuing addiction treatment and recovery, often report:

- Being in recovery is the best thing I ever did.
- I'm so relieved to find there are alternatives to prescription painkillers for chronic pain.
- I never knew life could be so joyful.
- Instead of wasting every day getting high, I contribute in meaningful ways.
- I'm so grateful for my new life in recovery.
- When I look back, I can't believe I behaved the way I did.
- The ripple effect of my behavior is now positive, rather than harmful.
- I have my integrity back.
- I admit when I make mistakes.
- Every morning, I work from a clean slate; I take care of resentments before they take care of me.
- You can't afford not to get help; if you commit to the idea, you'll find a way.

- Drugs and alcohol only masked my problems; recovery taught me how to face them.
- My life is full again.
- I have made so many warm and wonderful friendships in recovery; I'm no longer lonely.

These lists could go on and on. But you get the picture. Excuses stem from deeply ingrained beliefs that we tend not to question. But relying on old thinking keeps us stuck. When we look a little closer at our beliefs, we become open to new and refreshing alternatives. Sometimes that's all it takes to move out of the chaos and into the solution. Albert Einstein said it best: "We can't solve problems by using the same kind of thinking we used when we created them."

Other Factors That Interfere with Recognizing/ Identifying the Problem

Aside from well-meaning but misguided beliefs of family, other loved ones, and even professional health care providers, a couple other factors can keep older adults from getting the help they need.

Difficult to diagnose: Substance abuse in an older adult can be difficult to diagnose. Many of the symptoms overlap, including loss of balance, forgetfulness, and slurred speech. Even withdrawal symptoms can be mistaken for signs of aging.

Hiding the truth: Older adults who have become addicted to either a prescription drug or alcohol do a pretty darn good job of keeping their addiction a secret. For older adults, addiction brings forth images of drunkards and junkies in dark alleys—not images of themselves contentedly living in a retirement community. To identify as an addict or alcoholic would cause many older adults to swell with an unbearable amount of shame. And so they hide the truth until they are caught up in a full-blown addiction and suffer a fall or a DUI—a consequence serious enough to get the attention of health care professionals, the authorities, or loved ones. Older women who outlive spouses and live alone find their situation especially conducive to concealing how much alcohol they drink.

Accept and Adjust

Recognizing and accepting that your loved one's behavior has changed is paramount. But what's key is how you adjust to it. To adjust adequately, you have to take your first thoughts and gut reactions a step further. Unless your loved one ends up in the legal or medical system, where he or she is accurately assessed and diagnosed with dementia or another disorder, polypharmacy, or addiction, you might not recognize the extent of the problem. You have to discover what's really happening—what behaviors, exactly, are you adjusting to? Is Mom getting dementia and needing a higher level of care? Or is it possible that Mom's painkiller medication is affecting her ability to think clearly? Until we know what's happening, we can't take action with any confidence because any steps we take might only exacerbate the problem. If Mom's dementia is the result of aging, upgrading her level of care makes sense. But if it's the result of benzodiazepine and oxycodone (even if taken at the prescribed dose), Mom needs help with drug-free pain and anxiety management, something that most likely won't get addressed adequately at an assisted-living facility or nursing home.

To get at the root of the problem, you need information. You need facts. The best way to get them is by paying attention: Through awareness, observation, monitoring, and conversation, you can start to piece together what's really happening to your loved one. So put on that deerstalker cap, light your pipe, and start deducing. It's time to play the role of Sherlock Holmes.

Awareness: What are the signs of aging? What are the signs of polypharmacy? What are the signs of addiction? Does addiction run in the family? Did Dad use drugs as a teenager or young adult? How many doctors does Mom see? What are their names and locations? What health conditions is Grandpa being treated for?

Observation: How many pills is Mom taking? How many drinks is she having? When she doesn't drink, does her behavior improve? Where does she fill her prescriptions? Are the labels on her prescription medication bottles from more than one pharmacy? Does Mom have any drug paraphernalia lying around the house? Has Mom lost interest in some of the activities that used to bring her joy? Does she seem out of character—more depressed, anxious, withdrawn, or secretive?

Monitoring: How regularly is Grandpa being monitored? If I'm not around, who can I get to monitor his behavior? How often does he go to the doctor? How much does he drink? Does he forget that he took his medication in the morning and then take it again at night?

Conversation: Casually ask your loved one questions about her drug use and her behaviors. How many pills is she taking? Is each of her doctors aware of what the others are prescribing? (The signs and symptoms of polypharmacy can mimic dementia.) Has she been drinking? How much? Has she been feeling okay? Does she notice a change in her behavior? Extend the conversation to others—neighbors, friends, spouses, relatives, and caregivers, if appropriate.

Armed with information, you can talk to your loved one's doctors and request a medication audit—the first, best, and easiest defense against polypharmacy and addiction.

MEDICATION AUDIT: THE BROWN BAG APPROACH

Medication audits are in everyone's best interest. Physicians pledge to "do no harm," while hospitals need to ensure that patients are getting the best care possible. Bad drug combinations or errors in drug dosage or type can increase the number of days a patient spends in the hospital. More important, they can cause major discomfort and lead to addiction. They can also be deadly. About seven thousand Americans die annually from medication errors. Granted, most of these deaths take place in critical care settings, where staff are working under pressure to keep patients alive and are more prone to making mistakes.[19] But medication errors extend beyond hospital walls into product labeling, packaging, dispensing, monitoring, and use. The truth is that mistakes happen, and they can be costly. Rather than put all our trust in the system, we're wise to order an audit.

The easiest way to start an audit is to use what's known as the brown bag approach. Gather up every single pill bottle, nasal spray, supplement, and anything else Mom takes—including OTC drugs such as aspirin and cough syrup, as well as vitamins and minerals—put them in a brown paper lunch bag, and bring them to the next family doctor appointment. If you have a relationship with a good neighborhood pharmacist who can help you sort through the medications, you can bring the medications to him or her. Have the pharmacist, doctor, or nurse practitioner go through and eliminate all old or expired medications and then enter the medication names into their database of medications.

The information you get from a medication audit can turn your loved one's life around. Once you have this information, you and your loved one's primary health care provider can review the results and consider the options.

It can be hard to distinguish between physical and mental signs of aging and signs of addiction. Family members are not always nearby to notice how many bottles of alcohol or pills Dad is consuming in a month. Understanding our own beliefs about addiction and aging helps too. If we find ourselves reluctant to help, we need to examine our thoughts about aging. Being left alone in a stupor sitting in a wheelchair is most likely not how your loved one pictured living out her life. As caregivers, it's our responsibility to find out the cause of the behavior and, if possible, do what we can to lead our loved one to a full and engaging life.

To be sure you fully grasp the monstrous effect of polypharmacy, let's look at polypharmacy and its potential impact on mental health more closely as we explore dementia and other mental health disorders in the next chapter.

■

CHAPTER 3

The Truth about Substance Misuse, Dementia, and Other Mental Health Disorders

Emily, sixty-eight years of age, hosted a little party for some houseguests. They had a lovely time, drank a glass or two of wine, enjoyed each other's company, and then everyone went off to bed.

The next morning, as usual, Emily awoke around 5:00 a.m. She was horrified when she went to her kitchen. She found eggs left out of the refrigerator, a burner still on, pots and pans in the sink, butter melting by the open burner, and other plates and utensils in various states of disarray. She was angry and highly insulted that after such a delicately prepared meal her guests would get up in the middle of the night, make an omelet, and leave her kitchen, which had been spotless at bedtime, in such condition.

Around 8:00 a.m., her guests appeared for morning coffee, and she said, "Well, I guess I didn't feed you enough last night. It looks like you had a great time."

Her friends looked at her oddly, and one asked, "What do you mean?"

"Well, you know, didn't you get up and cook an omelet in the middle of the night?"

"Absolutely not, but we did hear a lot of clanging and banging in the kitchen that kind of woke us sometime around two o'clock in the morning."

Red faced and embarrassed, our hostess excused herself, went to her bathroom, stared in the mirror, and looked horrified. "Are you going crazy?" she said to her image staring back at her. "Have you lost your mind?"

Yes, with absolutely no recollection—in a total blackout—she had gotten up in the middle of the night, prepared an omelet, and put her home and guests in danger by leaving the gas on.

An audit of Emily's medications was quite interesting. There were the usual suspects—Lipitor for her cholesterol, hormone replacement therapy, Xanax (which she only took occasionally when anxious), and Ambien to aid her when she could not sleep—none of which she took on a regular basis. There was also a bunch of supplements that she usually tried to take to keep her health optimal.

Xanax and Ambien should never be taken together, as the combination can slow the central nervous system down to a crawl, resulting in heart failure. On that evening, she took Xanax around dinnertime, when she was getting nervous about preparing a flawless meal for her guests. She took the Ambien at bedtime so that she'd get to sleep quickly and be able to get up early in the morning and bake muffins for breakfast. All quite innocent. Add to that a glass or two of wine at dinner and you get the very common phenomena of blackout, loss of memory, and sleepwalking. I've heard this story many times, and this one, though bizarre, is not unusual.

■

Few things are more frightening than the sense that you're losing your mind, as can happen when people begin noticing memory loss and confusion with age. Some people are conscious of the decline and try to cover it up; others aren't aware that something strange is happening to them. In the story above, Emily tries to cover up her blackout incident. She drops the conversation with her houseguests about the omelet and is left feeling shameful and even more confused. Instead of talking to her doctor or her family members, she takes another Xanax to calm her nerves.

On the flip side, few things are more painful than when your own mother doesn't recognize you. When we begin to see signs and symptoms of dementia in our parents, it's horrifying. Not only do we feel we're losing a parent, a pillar of strength and support for many, but also we can't fathom the consequences.

Dementia is a serious brain disease affecting 47 million people worldwide.[20] Type, cause, and progression vary. Alzheimer's disease, frontotemporal dementia, and dementia with Lewy bodies are just a few types of dementia. To complicate things further, people can suffer from more than one type of the disorder, a condition known as mixed dementia. As the disease progresses, the older adult and family members get more and more frustrated as they feel limited in what they can do, and caregiving gets complicated. Depending on the type of dementia, sufferers can become combative, wander away from home and not know how to get back, hallucinate, and not recognize family members and other once-familiar people. Treatment is limited; it can include medications such as Aricept and Exelon, which work to enhance memory function, but for most dementias there is no cure. The only sure bet is that, over the course of about a decade, dementia leads to death; the brain slowly deteriorates, losing some of its vital functions related to orientation and memory.

COMMON SIGNS AND SYMPTOMS OF DEMENTIA

The signs and symptoms of dementia, as well as the rate at which they progress, are unique to each individual. While some older adults have a "pleasant" dementia and are usually smiling and happy, others are often combative and difficult. The following is a list of the more commons signs:

- memory loss/forgetfulness
- impaired judgment

- poor reasoning
- inappropriate behavior
- loss of communication skills
- disorientation to time and place
- gait, motor, and balance problems
- lack of personal care and hygiene
- hallucinations, paranoia, agitation

Dementia in Disguise

For some, however, dementia isn't the slow death sentence it appears to be. At least fifty conditions, ranging from alcoholism to Parkinson's disease to slow-growing brain tumors, can mimic the signs and symptoms of dementia. These dementias are known as reversible dementia. In some cases, such as alcoholism, the condition itself causes the cognitive impairment by killing brain cells. In other cases, such as depression, it can be the medication prescribed to treat the disorder. In depression, the condition and the medication can work together to mimic dementia. When cognitive impairment is caused by something other than true dementia, and if it is caught before significant brain damage has occurred, the symptoms are reversible.

An alarming 9 percent of older adults suffer from reversible dementia.[21] What makes this so alarming is that the most common, most overlooked, and most preventable cause is likely polypharmacy, and the patients, their family members, and their doctors may never know.

Poly means "many" and *pharmacy* means "medication." When we say medications, we mean everything: prescription drugs; over-the-counter substances such as aspirin and allergy pills or sprays; herbal and other supplements; as well as alcohol, marijuana, and street drugs. Medication alters brain chemistry. It changes the way our bodies work, usually in an effort to relieve pain or prevent dangerous disease symptoms from getting out of control and allowing a heart attack or stroke, for instance. When used appropriately, medication can save lives. When misused, overprescribed, prescribed in toxic combinations, taken with alcohol or other mood-altering drugs, taken for too long, or taken in ignorance, medication can do more harm than good. To add insult to injury, some medications, even when taken responsibly, can mimic the signs and symptoms of dementia.

Americans are prolific prescription drug users, with more than 90 percent of people sixty-five or older using at least one medication per week, more than 50 percent using at least five medications per week, and 12 percent using ten or more medications per week.[22] Let's add up the pills for three common disorders in older adults: heart disease (aspirin, lisinopril, Coumadin, Lanoxin, Lasix), arthritis (ibuprofen, naproxen sodium, Mobic, oxycodone, cortisone), and depression and anxiety (Zoloft, Xanax). As you can see, it doesn't take much to reach five or ten pills a day. Add a scotch, a glass or two of wine, or a marijuana brownie or two, and the older adult has unwittingly created a toxic cocktail of substances capable of causing confusion, combativeness, and forgetfulness—signs and symptoms of dementia.

Types of Drugs That Can Mimic Dementia

It doesn't matter whether the drugs are mood altering or addictive or not. It's the type, the combination, or the number of drugs that counts. In a study involving people age sixty-five and older in Taiwan, researchers determined that polypharmacy increased the risk of dementia, especially in women. Older adults taking drugs for chronic cerebrovascular disease, kidney disease, diabetes mellitus, and hypertension were especially prone to dementia.[23] The drugs typically taken for these diseases are neither mood altering nor addictive, but they affect body chemistry.

PRESCRIPTION DRUGS THAT CAN CAUSE DEMENTIA-LIKE SYMPTOMS

Following is a list of drug categories. Each of the drugs in these categories can cause dementia-like symptoms. The number of drugs included in each category varies, but the total number of medications that can cause dementia-like symptoms on their own is in the hundreds. When any of these drugs combine, either with each other or with other drugs not on the list, the probability for experiencing dementia-like symptoms increases significantly.

- antidepressants
- antihistamines
- anti-Parkinson drugs
- antianxiety medications
- cardiovascular drugs
- anticonvulsants
- corticosteroids
- hypnotics
- narcotics
- sedatives
- stimulants

MEDICAL CONDITIONS THAT CAN CAUSE DEMENTIA-LIKE SYMPTOMS

In the list of physical disorders that follows, the condition itself—not necessarily the drugs prescribed to treat the condition—can lead family members to believe their loved one is suffering from Alzheimer's or another form of dementia.

- alcoholism

- mood disorders, such as depression, that occur before cognitive impairment
- sleep disorders
- neurodegenerative diseases such as Parkinson's and Huntington's
- central nervous system infections
- vitamin B deficiency due to low absorption
- brain tumors
- thyroid disorders
- hydrocephalus (water on the brain)
- subdural hematoma (bruising on the brain)

Polypharmacy: Effect on Mind and Body

Some of the simplest drugs, even OTC drugs like Benadryl, can greatly affect the mental status of older adults. Let's start with anticholinergic medications often used for diarrhea, which can produce a side effect like dry mouth to the extent that a person's speech sounds somewhat garbled. Add to that an OTC sleep aid that leaves the patient groggy and hung over in the morning so that there's lack of coordination, slowed reflexes, and increased risk of falling. Add to that medications that can blur vision and, of course, impair memory. Combining these side effects can produce a picture of dementia that may appear little different than the irreversible dementias of Alzheimer's or other medical processes.

The Older Body and Drugs

Dementia is not just a geriatric problem; neither is polypharmacy. An estimated 5 percent of dementia cases are what's known as early-onset dementia, or dementia that affects people under age sixty-five.[24] The cause is sometimes considered genetic, but dementia among younger adults who use psychiatric and chronic pain medications, as well as OTC supplements, is also a concern. But we don't typically hear about a connection between polypharmacy and dementia in young adults. So why is polypharmacy and dementia such a major problem with older adults? And why do women suffer more than men? The answer most likely has to do with the body's ability to absorb, distribute, and excrete drugs.

Metabolism is a collection of chemical processes that takes place within our cells. When the body metabolizes, it breaks down certain substances and forms others. In women and older adults, metabolism is generally slower. The liver, responsible for breaking down drugs, and the kidneys, responsible for excreting them, have slowed down. The result is that drugs stay in the body longer and accumulate, creating a toxic effect. Poor nutrition, dependence on feeding tubes, or difficulty swallowing can also affect how much or how little of a drug an older adult can absorb.

How drugs work in older adults has not been well studied, mostly because many older adults take medication needed to stay alive and taking someone off a medication regimen for research purposes would be unethical. But we do know that most drugs have side effects that can mimic other conditions (like dementia). It's not uncommon for someone who is prescribed an antipsychotic to then experience symptoms of Parkinson's, which leads the doctor to prescribe an anti-Parkinson's therapy, which then causes orthostatic hypotension (low blood pressure brought about by sitting or lying down) and delirium. The list of drugs and the conditions they can mimic is endless, as is the number of prescriptions a doctor can write once caught up in the prescribing cascade. As we've seen, older adults, who often see multiple specialists, do not always share medication information with all of their attending physicians. The resulting polypharmacy can mimic conditions that call for more medications, cause serious cognitive impairment, or build up the level of toxins in a body that can no longer effectively process them.

When polypharmacy is the result of the right hand not knowing what the left hand is doing—when a person's doctors prescribe drugs to treat a condition or symptom and are unaware of how the patient is self-medicating with OTC drugs and supplements, as well as alcohol, marijuana, or other drugs, and do not know what the patient's other doctors have prescribed—the doctors are breaking their oath to "do no harm." By the same token, when patients are dishonest with their doctor about their alcohol and other drug intake, they put themselves in harm's way. In most cases, quality of life is markedly diminished. In some cases, people die.

Prevention

With all of these possibilities, it would seem impossible to get to the root cause of your loved one's memory loss and confusion—but it is possible. Whether an older adult's dementia is the result of drugs or another medical condition, there are steps you can take. The intention here is not to blame doctors. Patients and their family members have a responsibility to keep track of what patients are putting in their bodies. With older adults, however, tracking can get complicated. For the most part, they trust their doctors. They may not realize they have been taking their meds twice a day instead of once. They may live alone, their drug use unmonitored. Family members may be too busy to notice or unaware that the medications are a potential issue.

To find out whether an older adult's behaviors are medicine related, disease related, or true dementia—or to prevent polypharmacy from becoming an issue—you need information. Establish a personal health record for your loved one. Record all medications and dosages, along with the reasons they were prescribed. Search medicine cabinets for OTC medications, herbs, and supplements—everything from aspirin to calcium to ginkgo. Remember to also factor in drugs such as alcohol and marijuana. Go to doctor appointments with your loved one, and talk to the physicians about the medications and the older adult's health conditions. Show doctors your loved one's personal health record, and make sure they enter the information into their computer system so it becomes a permanent piece of your loved one's electronic health record and accessible to other physicians. Most important, talk to your loved one's doctors about whether polypharmacy could, either now or in the future, be affecting his or her mental health. If you sense that your concerns are not being taken seriously, get a second or even third opinion.

In addition, you can do some research on your own. The American Geriatric Society compiles what's known as the Beers list, or the American Geriatric Society's Beers Criteria for Potentially Inappropriate Medication Use in Older Adults, which is available at americangeriatrics.org. Review the medications your loved one is taking to ensure they are not on this list. The Beers list explains why these drugs are potentially dangerous for older adults. If your loved one is taking an inappropriate medication, discuss it with one or more doctors and dig into alternative and less invasive methods for dealing with the condition or symptom.

■

CHAPTER 4

Legally Crossing the Line: Painkillers, Sedative-Hypnotics, and Marijuana

Joseph and Tina, brother and sister, began to help care for their fifty-five-year-old mother, Joan, after she suddenly started acting oddly. At times, she seemed to be out of sorts, not with it, and forgetful, so they made a point to visit more often, clean the house, and cut the grass. Gradually her condition worsened, and one day they found her nearly catatonic.

These young people were completely flummoxed by their mother's condition. With their mother laid up in the emergency department, they searched through medicine cabinets and drawers and found dozens of prescription bottles and multiple prescriptions, some of them unfilled. They couldn't make heads or tails of this pile of pills. Several doctors were prescribing the same medications, and one or two doctors were prescribing six or seven medications. They put the pills in a brown bag and brought it to the hospital. Once Joan's physical condition was stable, the hospital referred her to the Betty Ford Center.

Joan had become addicted to pain medications and sedative-hypnotics. She had suffered from chronic pain for many years and frequented a pain clinic where doctors repeatedly refilled prescribed painkillers without necessarily reevaluating her pain status. She had been on painkillers for so long that she developed opioid-induced hyperalgesia, caused by a chronic escalation in her opioid dosage that created its own pain; the medication was now working against her and had begun to intensify her pain.

The Betty Ford Center did a complete medication audit and found that those medications most frequently used were the pain and sedative-hypnotic medications. They were mixed with her antihypertensive and diabetic medications, putting her in grave danger of overdose and certainly explaining why she was "out of it."

After a thorough assessment, detoxification, and a twenty-eight-day stay in our residential treatment unit, Joan and the kids learned to live by a whole new set of rules and guidelines regarding outside consultation and ongoing pain management. One doctor is serving as the gatekeeper for all other doctors, and any prescription must be filtered through him for appropriateness and compatibility with other medications before it can be filled. This is the way it should be.

■

Sedative-hypnotic drugs, which include Amytal, Ativan, and Xanax, as well as prescription painkillers such as OxyContin, Vicodin, and Percocet, are the main culprits when it comes to drug abuse and the older adult. As of this writing, the effects of medical marijuana are largely unknown, but we will also briefly look at the drug as a painkiller.

The vast majority of older adults innocently begin taking drugs based on doctor's orders. They most often are looking to ease symptoms of pain, anxiety, depression, or sleeplessness. And the regimen prescribed often works, at least initially. But somewhere along the way, normal use of the psychoactive drugs listed above quickly, easily, and inadvertently turns to abuse for 17 percent of older adults, which can lead to an untimely death via overdose or other complications. Consider that from 2004 to 2008, emergency departments saw a 121 percent increase in visits involving prescription medication misuse by older adults. Approximately 25 percent of older adults use prescription psychoactive medications that have the potential for misuse. The combination of alcohol and medication misuse is estimated to affect 19 percent of older adults. And perhaps most alarming is that nonmedical use of prescription drugs among older adults is expected to increase by 190 percent—from 911,000 in 2001 to 2.7 million in 2020.[25]

At times, taking mood-altering painkillers, such as Percocet, medical marijuana, or a nightly tranquilizer, seems to be the only way our loved ones are able to live comfortably. Before I address this conundrum, let's look at how prescription painkillers and sedative-hypnotics are creating a different kind of pain and discomfort among older adults.

Sedative-Hypnotics

Sedative-hypnotic drugs are the most widely abused class of drugs among older adults. Sedative-hypnotics include sleeping pills, tranquilizers, and sedatives. These drugs depress the brain and central nervous system and calm the body. More and more older adults are being prescribed sedative-hypnotics to help them sleep more soundly or to relieve symptoms of anxiety.

Barbiturates and benzodiazepines are the two major categories of sedative-hypnotic drugs. See the following chart for a partial list of some generic and brand names. The "unspecified" column in the chart lists very old and dangerous drugs that are off the market. If a doctor is prescribing them, find a new doctor. The only drug listed in the unspecified column that's worth noting is alcohol, a semihypnotic drug.

Sedative-Hypnotic Drugs[26]

Barbiturates *—helps put you to sleep*	**Benzodiazepines** *—helps relieve anxiety*	**Unspecified**
secobarbital (Seconal)	diazepam (Valium)	methaqualone (Quaalude)
pentobarbital (Nembutal)	lorazepam (Ativan)	ethchlorvynol (Placidyl)
	quazepam (Doral)	chloral hydrate (Noctec)
	alprazolam (Xanax)	meprobamate (Miltown)
	chlordiazepoxide (Librium)	alcohol
	chlorazepate (Tranxene)	

For the majority of people, taking a sedative-hypnotic drug occasionally for a better night's sleep is not an issue. However, long-term use can be habit forming. The effects can be amplified (and even deadly) when using a sedative with alcohol. An additional issue with older adults is the frequent need to go to the bathroom in the middle of the night. Confusion, disorientation, and problems with balance as a result of the drug can cause falls that result in serious injuries.

As mentioned earlier, most older adults do not intentionally abuse sedative-hypnotic drugs. Typically, they may not read the directions properly, especially when multiple prescriptions are involved. Or they may not understand that they cannot drink alcohol while on the drug. Also, they may have several physicians prescribing different medications who aren't aware that the drugs are being combined. Regardless, addiction and overdose can result, especially if the older adult continues to use the drug not as prescribed.

Prescription Painkillers

Nationwide, an estimated six million people of all ages and backgrounds abuse prescription painkillers, and according to the National

Institute on Drug Abuse, an alarming sixteen thousand people died in 2013 from opioid overdose, more than from any other drug. That same year, eight thousand people died from heroin use.[27]

A growing number of older adults engage in nonmedical use of prescription painkillers—they take the medications solely for their mood-altering effects.[28] Instead of legally refilling a prescription, they take from others, visit multiple pharmacies, network with other older adults in their apartment building, convince their doctor to give them a higher dose, or buy painkillers online or off the street.

In desperation, a small percentage might turn to heroin (which is also an opioid and falls into the same class of drugs as painkillers). Heroin is stronger and often less expensive; as of this writing, it has become more readily available than painkillers. Heroin use is far more common among young people, but older adults, especially those who may have had issues with drugs earlier in life, are vulnerable as well. Heroin is just as addictive but potentially even more dangerous because the buyer never really knows what he is getting. Bad drug combinations and unknown dosages, especially of the really pure heroin more commonly available now, can lead to overdose and death.

WHAT ARE OPIOIDS?

Prescription painkillers fall into a class of drugs known as opioids. They include codeine, fentanyl, hydrocodone, hydromorphone, meperidine, morphine, oxycodone, and tramadol. These drugs are sold under various brand names. For instance, hydrocodone might be sold under the brand name Vicodin. Other well-known brand names are Dilaudid (hydromorphone) and Demerol (meperidine). OxyContin, Percocet, and Percodan are all brand names for oxycodone.

Traditionally, the term *opiates* referred to substances occurring naturally in opium, a drug made from the opium poppy. Natural opiates include codeine and morphine. The term *opioids* traditionally referred to synthetic (laboratory-made) painkillers, including fentanyl and tramadol, that possess many of the same properties as natural opiates. Drugs made from a combination of natural opiates and synthetic substances are called semisynthetic opioids (or semisynthetic opiates). These drugs include heroin, oxycodone, and hydrocodone. *Opioids* is an umbrella term that includes opiates, yet many doctors do not make a distinction between these different terms.

We can also refer to both legal and illegal opioids as narcotics, a term that comes from the Greek word *narcos* meaning anything that makes a person sleepy.

Since the late 1990s, the nonmedical use of prescription painkillers has experienced a dramatic—and devastating—rise among most age groups. Since 2002, use of prescription painkillers has doubled. The result: From 1998 to 2008, the number of people of all ages treated for opioid abuse increased by 400 percent.[29] As you learned in the previous chapter, any drug—mood altering or not—can cause issues when combined with other medications. The United States is by far the largest consumer of opioids, using about 80 percent of the supply worldwide.[30]

These numbers do not reflect just a trend but a heartbreaking epidemic that is ruining the lives of millions of people and their families. It used to be that almost everyone could say they knew an alcoholic, either a friend, coworker, family member, or distant relative. Now it's safe to say that almost everyone knows someone who is struggling or has struggled with opioid dependency. The best way to stop the insanity is to closely monitor prescription opioid use for acute pain (surgery, dental work, broken bones) and to find other viable ways to approach the chronic pain conundrum.

If abuse of mood-altering prescription medications can happen so easily, why then are doctors putting patients at risk by writing prescriptions?

How Did We Get Here?: The Fifth Vital Sign

For years, doctors avoided prescribing opioids to treat chronic pain for fear that patients would too easily get addicted. It had happened before. Heroin, unregulated at the turn of the nineteenth century, was used in cough medicine and prescribed for assorted ailments into the 1920s. Heroin use again saw an increase through the 1950s and 1960s in the United States. In the midst of that wave, in 1961, the United Nations declared that access to pain medication was a basic human right. Still, doctors were cautious, fearing that chronic pain patients would easily get addicted to painkillers.

In the 1980s, studies began to show that only a small percentage of people actually became addicted to opioid painkillers. The mind-set in the medical community began to soften, and by the mid-1990s, physicians acknowledged that too many people were suffering from untreated pain. If the likelihood of addiction was low, maybe patients were being undertreated. Physicians underwent a paradigm shift when they included pain as the fifth vital sign: They took your temperature, blood pressure, and pulse; checked your respiration rate; and then asked you, on a scale of 1 to 10 (or by looking at a chart with a series of faces that start with a big smile and gradually cascade into a major frown), how intense your pain was. If you were suffering from back pain, a broken bone, nerve pain, cancer, or any other number of conditions and indicated that your pain level was 6 or higher (the point at which the smile turned to a frown), your doctor was pretty much obligated to give you a prescription for OxyContin, Percocet, or any one of the many opioid painkillers available on the market.

As an active physician in family medicine and primary care from the mid-1970s on, I well remember the precautions that were unnecessarily given to physicians regarding controlled substances. I completely agree that pain was undertreated. The main problem was not in using narcotics to treat acute pain but the duration pain prescriptions were used, renewed, and ultimately abused by patients. Physician awareness, or lack of it, was of key importance here. Oftentimes, staff members and associates refilled prescriptions, and the physician didn't know that a patient was getting two, three, four, or five refills on a significantly addictive pain medication. So prescribing narcotics got a bad rap—until not treating pain got an even bigger rap.

In the 1990s, treating pain became a requirement. Undertreated pain is a legally compensable event. So now physicians were held responsible for patients' pain and suffering when they were under treatment, which further contributed to the shift in the pendulum requiring that a pain level of 6, 7, or 8 be treated—which meant painkillers were much more liberally prescribed.

Acute pain often subsides in a day or two, so the patient winds up having a large supply of leftovers. Saving them for a rainy day, people store these very powerful drugs in bedroom drawers, night tables, and medicine cabinets. Down the road, Grandma might share her pain medicine with a friend or family member who sprained an ankle. Or, worse, Grandma's grandson or granddaughter might pillage the house looking for leftover narcotics. These pills are like candy to some young people, who attend "pharming" parties, where all sorts of mood-altering pills are thrown into a bowl and mixed together. Unsuspecting youths blindly grab a couple of pills, not knowing what they're taking and not grasping that some combinations are deadly, and wash them down with alcohol. The lucky ones vomit. Others end up in the emergency room. This deadly and dangerous game, played mostly by twelve- to twenty-year-olds, starts with a legal prescription.

Initially, at least, people make choices about what pills they put in their bodies, but a great deal of the responsibility must sit squarely with the prescribing physicians who often prescribe far too many medications and renew prescriptions far too readily. Some doctors felt safe doing this based on pharmaceutical company claims that the drugs were safe to use over long periods of time. In recent years, lawsuits against and large fines placed on pharmaceutical manufacturers have put an end to some of the false claims. By then, however, the epidemic was in full swing.

The truth is that acute pain needs to be treated adequately for short periods, often one to three days after a surgery, a tooth extraction, or an ankle sprain or other injury, and then be decreased or tapered to a nonaddictive medication. Ancillary treatments such as ice, compresses to control painful swelling, elevation, and rest and rehabilitation should be amply used. These directives, however, often take time to explain to patients and, in overcrowded offices, are sometimes overlooked. This is not an excuse but an explanation. Chronic pain is another story.

The Painkiller Paradox: How Painkillers Actually Work

Mood-altering painkillers were always meant to be a temporary solution and for good reason. Painkillers, it turns out, can actually cause pain.

When you sprain an ankle, break a bone, cut a finger, or have a backache or headache, special nerve endings called nociceptors send messages to your brain, telling it in no uncertain terms that you are hurt and need help. In response, the brain sends out "feel-good" neurotransmitters such as endorphins to ease the pain. The brain may increase the blood flow to the injured area causing some swelling, redness, and tenderness. But this also allows for the transport of the healing cells in the blood—white blood cells in the case of infection, osteoblasts and osteoclasts in the case of fractures—into the injured area. In the case of a sports injury, for example, muscles on either side of an injury may go into spasm, creating their own pain but actually functioning as a splint on a sprained or fractured area. This splinting is very appropriate to keep the parts in place and prevent painful excess motion, until proper immobilization, casting, or internal fixation of the injury can happen.

Painkillers, including everything from aspirin, ibuprofen, and acetaminophen to morphine and other opioids, are designed to block the messages nociceptors are sending before they reach the brain. In effect, you still have the injury or the headache, but your brain doesn't know it so you don't perceive it.

On some level, pain is a good thing. It tells you that your body needs attention. If you have a swollen ankle and feel pain when you put pressure on it, you're much less likely to go for a run and exacerbate the problem. If your nerve endings didn't communicate with your brain, you wouldn't perceive the pain, and you'd be prone to causing more damage.

Once you know your pain needs attention, painkillers can come in handy. Taking non-mood-altering painkillers such as aspirin for headaches and other minor aches and pains (as needed and at proper dosages) is relatively harmless. These pills can damage the liver, but this happens only after long-term use. Surgeries, severe injuries, and other highly painful circumstances require something a little stronger—the best-known solution to date is narcotics.

Narcotic painkillers have their place in the world of health care. In addition to numbing or masking physical pain, they take a lot of fear out of going through medical procedures, and they make healing a lot more relaxing and attractive. There's a reason morphine is still used in operating rooms nearly two hundred years after the powerful opioid was first isolated and sold commercially. It works. It works very well.

If used properly and for the necessary duration, mood-altering painkillers save us from experiencing what would in some cases be torturous pain. If used too long, however, these strong medications can begin to damage our endorphin receptor sites and create a condition known as opioid-induced hyperalgesia. With this condition, when nerve endings send pain signals to the brain, the pain medication blocks them and sends out its own endorphins, but the receptor sites have been damaged from "over use." We perceive the pain, but we don't get to feel any relief. By damaging our "feel-good" receptor sites, painkillers leave us with no way to alleviate the pain—neither naturally nor through narcotics.

If we suffer from rheumatoid arthritis or severe osteoarthritis, for example, our nerve endings might send never-ending messages to the brain, creating an ongoing, or chronic, pain. In these cases, continued use of painkillers is common, leaving endorphin receptors in a shambles and negating any positive effects. The painkillers, in other words, stop working and leave the body unable to fend for itself.

Opioid painkillers can create chronic pain by damaging the brain's feel-good chemical receptor sites. The patient perceives pain and takes higher and higher doses of the narcotic in an effort to relieve the pain, which only aggravates the receptor sites further and does not give them a chance to repair themselves. The longer the patient takes narcotics and the more of them the patient takes, the more likely he or she is to get addicted, adding pain of a different kind.

The Pain in Painkillers: Addiction and Low Recovery Rates

In 2015, the U.S. Department of Health and Human Services acknowledged that about 2.5 million people needed treatment for opioid dependence but that less than half were getting it.[31] In response, the government loosened control of access to two important drugs currently being used to treat opioid dependence: buprenorphine and naloxone. Both are used in what's known as medication-assisted treatment (MAT), an evidence-based model of care that's been around since the early 2000s but that has been sorely underutilized, partly because the government has limited the supply of medications.

Buprenorphine works as a kind of maintenance program, much like methadone only easier to administer because doctors can write a prescription. Naloxone, carried by many first responders, blocks opioid receptors in the brain and can be injected to prevent an overdose. It also takes the pleasure out of using narcotics, which has the effect of reducing cravings.

Although it's an epidemic, addiction to painkillers is grossly undertreated and underdiagnosed. When people do seek treatment, recovery rates can be dismal, in part because the early withdrawal symptoms can create behaviors that are hard to manage in early recovery. Patients may go from feeling no pain at all to experiencing magnified pain sensations throughout their bodies. They can feel hopeless and resist treatment. MAT is, however, proving somewhat effective in certain circumstances. I'm not a fan of long-term MAT, but I am a fan of prolonged detoxification and support when necessary and in certain cases.

Under no circumstances should anyone have to detoxify from pain medications or any other opioid alone. County detox programs are available throughout the country for little or no cost, if finances are an issue. Withdrawal from pain meds is uncomfortable and dangerous if not supervised by medical professionals who can monitor symptoms, administer helpful medications, and taper withdrawal.

Beyond Complacency

As caregivers and loved ones, we need to challenge our paradigm for painkiller use. Of course we want our loved ones to be comfortable in old age. We don't want them to suffer—so why would we substitute one painful situation for another?

In an effort to help those suffering from pain, we've created a new and deadly scenario that has resulted in the national epidemic of painkiller misuse and addiction. It's insane. But in response to the insanity, a host of new (and ancient) ways to manage pain has arisen, which I will talk about in detail in chapter 11.

For now, I want to emphasize the importance of keeping perspective. Painkillers, and even medical marijuana, can serve as a temporary solution to help alleviate pain. No one should have to suffer needlessly. But prescription painkiller use requires monitoring. If your loved one is in pain and not currently taking anything, consider all options. Following are suggestions for what to do if your loved one is taking painkillers:

If your loved one is taking painkillers but shows no sign of being addicted, he or she may have simply built up a tolerance to the medication. This may delude everyone into thinking that a higher dose is necessary. The prescribing physician signs on with this plan so that the next refill is filled early or the quantity dispensed is increased. At the Betty Ford Center, we see this kind of escalation in the written prescription all the time. Remember that people need not behave like stereotypical addicts to be addicted: They're not buying their drugs on the street, trying to get them off the Internet, or running out of their prescriptions early; they are taking the medications exactly as prescribed. Yet they may indeed be quite dependent on the medication, and if it were interrupted or the dosage decreased, they likely would go through very significant withdrawal symptoms. Sometimes the first sign of dependence and addiction is the withdrawal symptoms that happen when a prescription doesn't get refilled in a timely fashion. You can get a hint by the anxiety that the patient displays or his preoccupation with the next dose: "I must have my pills set out for me; I won't wait one minute past the time, set the alarm clock; refill my prescription a week early so I don't run out."

If your loved one is beginning to show signs of addiction, this is the time to discuss your concerns with the prescribing physician. Even if the physician knows nothing about addiction, your concerns will raise a red flag in the office of the prescriber. And everyone will and should be on the lookout for the patient's welfare. The clinic could flag a patient's chart to be cautious about prescribing amounts and frequency, suggest a face-to-face visit with the prescriber with family members there as well, or require a conversation between doctor and patient. You could even initiate a discussion without mentioning the worry about addiction by asking whether the combination of medications decreases the efficiency of the pain medication so it's not giving the needed relief. In any of these situations, eventually a really smart primary care physician will seek the advice of an addiction medicine specialist and/or a geriatric specialist and do a medication audit, address chronic pain issues differently, identify dependence, and treat it appropriately.

If your loved one is clearly addicted, he or she most likely needs detoxification and treatment, which will be discussed later in this book, specifically designed for older adults with chronic pain and other common co-occurring conditions, such as chronic anxiety, depression, or insomnia. Depending on the physical and mental condition of your loved one, a brief intervention, detoxification, and inpatient or outpatient addiction treatment might be necessary. Start by talking to the family doctor. Ask to be referred to a doctor or counselor certified in addiction medicine where you can get the support and answers you need.

What If My Loved One's Physician Wants to Prescribe Painkillers?

For acute pain, ask the physician to prescribe a minimal amount of painkillers, to create a tapering plan before they're prescribed, to monitor the patient closely, and to identify alternatives to use when appropriate. Physical therapy, ice, and other ancillary treatments can help the patient with pain. Bring a physical therapist into the home if you can. Movement greatly reduces pain in the long run and is a requirement for chronic pain patients.

For chronic pain in older adults, I would also consider getting a physiatrist, or physical medicine specialist, involved. I do not like to see patients work with pain management centers that run pill mills and spend little time with the patients and even less time looking for the development of dependence and addiction.

If the physician doesn't cooperate, put him or her on notice that you will actively look for a different doctor who understands your concerns.

What If My Mom's Physician Wants to Prescribe a Sedative-Hypnotic Drug?

If your loved one's doctor wants to prescribe a sedative-hypnotic medication, be upfront and straightforward about your concerns. Tell the physician, "If you give my mother a sedative or drug that doesn't mix well with other drugs, and she slips or falls or burns the house down, our family is going to hold you responsible." It's that simple. If the doctor doesn't comply or gets huffy, ask for your loved one's medical records and go elsewhere. If your mother is firmly invested in that doctor, then you have to be very careful and speak privately with the doctor about your concerns and how she acts. If the doctor insists on using these medications, you may have to request that your older adult stay in a facility where staff will be able to watch her more closely than you could at home. Alternatives always exist for pain medication and relaxation. Do not put your loved one at risk for falls and injury or addiction.

PREVENTING FALLS

When children fall, they seem to bounce right up and shake it off. That's not the case with older adults. Falls are a serious issue in older adults and can lead to broken bones, hospitalization, and rehabilitation in a nursing home. According to the Centers for Disease Control and Prevention (CDC), adults who are sixty-five and older are especially vulnerable to falls. In fact, millions of older adults fall each year, resulting in significant injuries, including broken bones and concussions.

The CDC estimates that one in three older adults will fall, and falling once doubles a person's chance of falling again.[32] Older adults report less than half of these falls to their doctors. Once a person falls, he may begin to reduce daily activities, which further weakens his physical strength and balance. This, in turn, sets up the person for another fall.

Some of the risk factors that contribute to falls include vision problems, foot pain, and medications that cause dizziness or sleepiness. Some ways to offset these risks include having a vision examination, doing strength-building exercises, and having a doctor evaluate medications for negative effects.

The CDC has a helpful online program called STEADI—Stopping Elderly Accidents, Deaths & Injuries. This free resource is available on the CDC website.

What If My Parent Is Considering Using Medical Marijuana to Kill Pain?

Marijuana is an issue that should be taken up with patients and their primary care physician. Marijuana does indeed work for some people in very limited circumstances, for those with chronic pain or glaucoma for instance, and may be a less harmful alternative to long-term pain management. Although it has very significant effects on the respiratory system, it could be taken orally in some patients to relieve pain that is otherwise intractable.

Medical marijuana has been around for more than five thousand years. It is a viable painkiller. It works. I don't like its method of delivery in smoking form because it causes lung damage, cough, and respiratory difficulties. In addition, it's not easily dosed because it's not standardized—and it's much more powerful that the marijuana of the 1960s. However, if medical marijuana helps someone's glaucoma or reduces chronic pain or chemotherapy nausea in a cancer patient, I'm all for it, but I advocate for small doses and, when possible, taken in the oral form called Marinol, which seems to get around some of the dosing complications.

Many people want to use medical marijuana just to get high and don't find any real therapeutic value in using it. For some older adults, marijuana may be their drug of choice, and with more states decriminalizing marijuana possession and legalizing medical and recreational use of marijuana, misuse and even addiction is sure to be a growing problem. With recreational marijuana more readily available and much more potent than what was available to boomers in the 1960s and 1970s, loved ones will need to monitor an older adult's use of this drug, especially as it becomes a factor in polypharmacy. Many people still think that marijuana isn't an addictive drug but it is, and when misuse becomes habitual, it's important to look for signs of addiction and get professional help for those you care for.

All mood-altering drugs are adept at hijacking the brain, creating a situation in which the user has no control. The next chapter covers exactly what happens to the brain when drugs take over—how drugs create dependency. In chapter 11, I talk about how to kill pain safely, by either monitoring mood-altering drug use or using non-mood-altering methods.

■

CHAPTER 5

Addiction: It's a Disease

Throughout this book, addiction is referred to as a disease. How can we call what looks on the surface to be an intentional behavior—drinking in excess or popping pill after pill—a disease? Like other diseases, addiction has a target organ and produces a set of symptoms. In the case of addiction, the target organ is not expendable, like an appendix. Addiction takes control of the brain.

The Disease Concept

Disease is defined as a loss of function of an organ or organ system. A disease also has a cause and an effect, producing symptoms. The pancreas, for example, is a target organ for diabetes. Diabetes is the result of a dysfunction in insulin production or in insulin's action at the cellular level. The effect is that the body becomes glucose intolerant, resulting in high blood sugar levels that, over time, wreak havoc on the entire body.

Diabetes is a chronic, lifelong, incurable but treatable disease. A patient with diabetes can keep it at bay by following a daily regimen, directing special attention toward diet, exercise, and medication in an effort to normalize blood sugar levels. But if left untreated, the chronic elevated blood sugar levels associated with diabetes ultimately cause heart disease, nerve damage, kidney disease, and blindness. If the diabetic adheres to his daily regimen, however, these consequences are usually preventable. In fact, the diabetic can live a long life looking and feeling healthier than most of the rest of the population, if only because he is taking healthy measures to keep the disease at bay. But if left untreated, diabetes is a fatal disease. As we'll see, addiction is a chronic disease as well that is fatal if left untreated.

The Disease Concept Applied to Addiction

Throughout history, alcoholism and drug addiction were thought to be anything but a disease. Most people believed that drinking until all hours of the night, shooting up morphine, or spending the day passed out in an opium den was simply a matter of choice and a moral failing. But research has proven history to be wrong.

PERCEPTION OF DRUG USE IN THE UNITED STATES: A BRIEF HISTORY

Some drugs that are considered taboo in modern times were commonplace in colonial America and the early United States. Apothecary shops, or pharmacies, routinely sold tonics and elixirs containing opium, morphine, and marijuana. The products were touted as treatments for a variety of health complaints, including pain, insomnia, "female problems," and stomach ailments. They were not subject to government regulation, and their manufacturers were not required to list ingredients on the label. A famous example is Mrs. Winslow's Soothing Syrup, first manufactured in the 1840s. Concocted by two druggists from Bangor, Maine, the syrup was said to soothe the pain of teething infants. Its two primary ingredients were morphine and alcohol.

Administered with the newly invented hypodermic needle and syringe, morphine eased the pain of wounded soldiers during the Civil War. By the end of the war, in 1865, an estimated four hundred thousand veterans were addicted to the drug. Meanwhile, San Francisco, Denver, and other western U.S. cities saw the emergence of opium dens, where primarily

Chinese immigrants but also some native-born Americans smoked opium for pleasure—a practice that led to addiction for many.

Although U.S. reformers decried opium addiction, labeling it a moral failing, manufacturers continued to include opium and other addictive drugs in patent medicines. In Atlanta, Georgia, Dr. John Stith Pemberton created Pemberton's French Wine Coca—a mixture of wine and cocaine—which he marketed as a cure-all. When some parts of Georgia banned the sale of alcohol in the mid-1880s, Pemberton replaced the wine in his drink with sweet syrup and changed the name to Coca-Cola. Another popular product was heroin, first processed in Germany by the Bayer Company in the 1890s. It was sold as a safe remedy for pneumonia, tuberculosis, and other respiratory diseases.

But it soon became clear that heroin, cocaine, and other drugs were addictive. Due to concerns about drug abuse, in 1903 Coca-Cola removed the cocaine from its drink. In 1906, the U.S. Pure Food and Drug Act required that makers of patent medicines label their ingredients, which led many manufacturers to drop the addictive ingredients altogether. Additional U.S. laws put an end to the free and legal use of addictive drugs. For instance, the Harrison Narcotics Act of 1914 made opiates and cocaine available by prescription only. The 1924 Heroin Act made it illegal to manufacture heroin. Even as the authorities cracked down on drug use, Americans continued to make, sell, and use addictive drugs, but now they did so clandestinely, aware that their actions could get them arrested.

In the 1970s, the U.S. government initiated a campaign to cut off the multimillion-dollar drug trade in which gangs produced heroin, cocaine, and methamphetamine in Mexico and South American countries and sold them across the United States. This so-called "War on Drugs" has resulted in the mass incarceration of small-time dealers and users of illegal drugs, many of them minorities with no other criminal record.

Since the 1950s, solid research has led most medical professionals and laypeople alike to understand that addiction is not a moral issue but a complex brain disease with genetic links. The National Institute on Alcohol Abuse and Alcoholism, the National Institute on Drug Abuse, and the Substance Abuse and Mental Health Services Administration continue to do important research on addiction in hopes of better understanding how and why it afflicts an estimated 10 percent of the population, while others can take or leave alcohol and other drugs without a second thought.

THE PROOF

Following is a truncated chronology of research that has advanced our understanding of addiction and how it works:

1956: Researchers identify "pleasure centers" in the lateral hypothalamus.

1963: Researchers "map" the reward sites, or pleasure centers, in a rat's brain.

1982: Dr. Roy A. Wise establishes the dopamine hypothesis of addiction—dopamine encourages drug use and, during early sobriety, the lack of drug-induced dopamine renders people unable to enjoy normal everyday pleasures.

1993: Research redefines dopamine as a reward neurotransmitter, giving users an incentive (reward in the form of good feelings, or highs) for using the same drug (the drug of choice).

2000: Dr. A. Thomas McLellan publishes a paper comparing addiction with common medical diseases, positioning addiction as a chronic disease.

2002: Dr. G. Alan Marlatt confirms that cognitive-behavioral therapy can help prevent relapse.

2006: The National Institute on Alcohol Abuse and Alcoholism conducts the National Epidemiologic Survey on Alcohol and

Related Conditions, the largest study ever to examine substance use and mental health disorders, leading to improved treatment methods specific to co-occurring disorders.

The medical community has given us proof: Addiction is a disease. Yet many people—often older adults who grew up believing that addiction is a moral failing—find this fact hard to accept. And that's understandable. Many addicts and alcoholics, after all, can be less than amiable when seeking their drug of choice. They can put families in turmoil, create an avalanche of stress that suffocates those around them, and leave loved ones feeling on the brink of insanity. If you've ever encountered addiction in a loved one, you know I'm not exaggerating. But however hard addiction is on everyone it touches, it is not ultimately a moral failing. Addiction is a brain disease with signs and symptoms, manifested in part as behaviors. And like diabetes, addiction has a target organ, a cause, and an effect.

Addiction and the Brain

When a wolf pounces on its prey, it goes straight for the jugular. The vein, full of life-sustaining blood, is closest to the surface of the neck and an easy target. Similarly, alcohol and other drugs head straight for the midbrain, the part of the brain most vulnerable to the effects of pleasure.

For our purposes, what's most important to know about the midbrain—also known as the survival, or reptilian, brain—is that it dictates survival behaviors, everything from breathing, eating, and voiding to procreating. Survival behaviors are instinctive. We're driven to do them without a whole lot of analysis, which takes place in a different part of the brain called the cortex. Survival behaviors require reinforcement not logic. Nature's goal is that we as a species survive, and our midbrain helps us meet that evolutionary goal by releasing dopamine, a "feel-good" neurotransmitter, every time we do something that encourages survival instead of death or extinction. When we're parched, we seek water, knowing how good those first gulps will feel. When we experience orgasm through sexual intercourse, we're encouraged to procreate. These pleasurable feelings are directly related to the midbrain, which encourages us to repeat behaviors that feel good and to avoid those that don't.

As if heading for the jugular, alcohol and other drugs attack the midbrain. Their weapon is not jaws but dopamine—and lots of it. According to the National Institute on Drug Abuse, some drugs release two to ten times more dopamine than natural rewards such as eating or cuddling a baby. At first, the influx of dopamine can feel better and stronger and last longer than the body's natural reward system. The brain, fooled by dopamine's evil twin, rewards us for using drugs.

But not for long . . .

Eventually, the brain adjusts to being periodically flooded with dopamine. It produces less and less of the neurotransmitter or even shuts down some of its dopamine receptor sites in an effort to control dopamine levels. This is the point where a drinker or drug user is "crossing the line." It's 5:00 p.m. and Dad (or rather Dad's midbrain) is conditioned to receive some dopamine from an external source. If Dad's late for happy hour, he starts feeling some anxiety. He needs a drink, and he needs it now. But he doesn't need it to feel high. At this point, he needs it to feel normal.

The point where a mood-altering drug hijacks the brain's reward system—when the source of dopamine is a drug rather than the pleasures associated with survival—is when addiction takes control. Via dopamine levels, addiction, like a wolf in sheep's clothing, tells the addict that drinking or using is as necessary to survival as breathing.[33]

Addiction keeps us drinking and drugging even when we don't want to, when we swear not to, and when we know our actions are hurting ourselves and our loved ones—even when we do things that are counter to our survival.

Logic, after all, is not part of the reptilian brain.

What Causes the Disease of Addiction?

Addiction is a complex disorder. Although its course is fairly predictable, each and every addict I've seen comes into treatment with a unique set of circumstances. The person who grew up in a household where his parents smoked marijuana, gave him permission to use drugs and alcohol at a young age, and gave him a case of wine for his high school graduation is going to be in trouble. By the same token, the kid who grew up with missionary parents, with no history in the family of chemical dependency, but who got exposed to medications like OxyContin and Vicodin when he broke his arm skateboarding at the age of fourteen may well be injecting heroin by the age of twenty. The backgrounds of these individuals are polar opposites, yet the result is the same.

Addiction, as it turns out, can have both genetic and environmental factors in its development. Let's return to diabetes as a disease metaphor. Diabetes type I is based on genetics, inherited traits passed down from generation to generation through DNA. Diabetes type II can also be genetic, but it is often triggered by consuming excessive amounts of sugar. Similarly, the disease of addiction is thought to be, on the average, about 60 percent genetic and 40 percent environmental.

A nine-year-old who lives in a home with a refrigerator always fully stocked with cola might be tempted to drink cola when thirsty. He likes the taste and, because he has a choice, he chooses it over water. Eventually, he's up to six colas a day and has put on twenty pounds in less than a year. His body now craves the sugar and caffeine. The child is soon diagnosed with type II diabetes. At this point, the child has effectively altered his body's chemistry. Like the nine-year-old type II diabetic who lives in a home with a refrigerator full of an unlimited supply of cola, the addict will take advantage of an environment where the refrigerator is stocked with beer instead.

We may carry the addiction genes, drink, and even use drugs occasionally, but never become addicted. To become an addict, we must first trigger the expression of our addiction genes. A person who has inherited these genes and grows up in a healthy environment with little or no exposure to drugs and alcohol, and who doesn't experience any major traumatic life events, may never manifest the disease. Is he still genetically an addict or an alcoholic? Yes, he has those chromosomal traits. But the environment has not supported the disease's development, at least not yet, so he can drink or take drugs without showing signs of addiction.

On the other hand, someone who hasn't seen addiction in her family since the Civil War, but who attends a high school where drugs are popular and accessible, might very well find herself trying pot, then beer, then tequila, and progressing to a potpourri of pills from painkillers to amphetamines until she ends up dropping out of school and stealing pills from Grandma's medicine cabinet. She's lost control over her ability to decide when and where to use. The midbrain has taken over, and she's now addicted.

Researchers have found that addiction genes can be triggered in three major ways: a traumatic life event, chronic stress, and repeated exposure to a mood-altering substance.

The Triple Threat

Addiction genes do not have an expiration date—they can be triggered at any time in life. For many older adults, the major triggers of trauma, chronic stress, and repeated exposure are a triple threat.

Trauma

Trauma doesn't cause addiction, yet at least 50 percent of addicts have a history of trauma, and that percentage might be as high as 90 percent for women.[34] According to psychologist Dr. Johanna O'Flaherty in her book *The Correlation between Trauma and Addiction*, "When people are traumatized, they are overpowered. They do not give their power away; it is taken from them. . . . Trauma is an event or a series of events that overwhelms our natural coping abilities." Trauma comes in many forms and can happen in expected and unexpected places: the battlefield, the schoolyard, the home. When we're traumatized, we become more reactive to stress, and so it's easy to turn to drugs or alcohol in an effort to numb uneasy feelings, including anxiety, depression, and fear. Trauma manifests itself as behavior.

Chronic Stress

When we're stressed out—in fight or flight mode—our adrenal glands release cortisol, a steroid hormone that helps control blood sugar levels and the inflammatory response, as well as immune function. Stress, by the way, can be "good" or "bad." We might be worried about planning our daughter's wedding (a happy stressor) or nervous about having enough funds to pay our taxes (a not-so-happy stressor). The body doesn't care about the source of our stress. All it knows is that we need cortisol and we need it now.

Occasional stress usually isn't a problem. It can serve us by helping us finish the landscaping and get the wedding invitations printed in time for our daughter's wedding, for instance. Stress is a problem when it becomes chronic. And many older adults have assorted stressors—physical and emotional—coming at them from every direction: chronic illness, disability, death of a spouse, financial hardship, loneliness, a move to a nursing home, and concern for what's going on in the lives of family members. Ongoing stress, or chronically high levels of cortisol, has detrimental effects on the body: It damages brain cells, leads to depression (which has its own set of harmful symptoms), increases memory loss, adversely affects digestion and glucose and cholesterol levels, and accelerates the overall aging process.

In addition to these physical symptoms, chronic stress reduces the number of opioid and dopamine receptor sites, in effect raising the dopamine requirements in the person who has the addiction genes—one in ten people in the United States.

Repeated Exposure to Alcohol or Other Drugs

The people who say they will never drink before 5:00 p.m. or will never have a drink at lunchtime may find that when their life circumstances change due to financial difficulties, job loss, or the death of a spouse, the floodgates suddenly open. Retirement is a huge reason for changing drinking or drugging patterns, as daily structure is, for many, reduced to a mere shadow of what it once was.

Once our dopamine requirements rise—whether from trauma, stress, or repeated exposure—normal pleasures no longer suffice. Even if we haven't had an ounce of alcohol in fifty years, or if we've always been content to drink socially, we suddenly find we "need a drink" to calm our nerves. Or we talk ourselves into taking one extra pill just to get to sleep tonight. Our midbrain has raised the dopamine bar, and our instinct is to find a way to cooperate with our survival brain's request.

RAISING THE BAR

Remember the carnival game where you hit a block with a big hammer, causing a weight to fly up a cable and ring a bell? Imagine that the bell being rung is a dopamine bell and that, to survive, you're required to ring it on a regular basis. You have no choice in the matter. If you want to breathe and eat and reproduce, you must pick up the hammer, hit the block, and ring the bell. Your shoulder is starting to hurt from all this bell ringing, so you take an opioid painkiller. You look up and see that the surge of dopamine in the form of a painkiller had the effect of raising the bell ten feet on the cable. Suddenly, the hammer, or those things that have caused pleasure in the past (delicious food, good sleep, satisfying sexual activity), isn't effective anymore. A bigger hammer is needed. Like more painkillers. Like cocaine. Like alcohol. The addictive substance trumps the normal behaviors that ring the bell and becomes a requirement for the bell ringing. Our midbrain is now sending out cravings for the substance that it deems necessary for survival—the amount of dopamine that comes from opioids. The midbrain will require us to seek out the same substance, over and over and over again, until the cycle is broken.

The Symptoms of Addiction

Each disease has a set of signs and symptoms. If a diabetic's blood sugar levels are off the charts, we can find her in a diabetic coma, unable to speak coherently. Likewise, addiction comes with a set of physical signs and symptoms. Physical symptoms can be from the harsh effect chronic drug use has on the body, such as cirrhosis of the liver, an enlarged spleen, a shrunken brain, bleeding from the mouth, high blood pressure, a hole in the lining of the nose, and much, much more.

But addiction has another layer of symptoms that is more about behaviors than ailments. The symptoms of addiction are not only biological but also emotional, social, and spiritual. Most of us call them consequences.

Emotionally, people who misuse alcohol or other drugs do it to numb uncomfortable feelings—everything ranging from boredom to anxiety—rather than deal with them. When misuse becomes addiction, when people can no longer control their use, addicts (and their families) are then on a roller coaster ride of depression, anxiety, anger, isolation, and mood swings. In older adults, you might see sleepiness, lack of attention, and blank stares. They may get agitated, obstreperous, and difficult. The guilt and shame over their inability to stop using is usually overwhelming, especially for alcoholics or addicts who believe they have failed morally.

Addiction is the great isolator. Unbearable feelings of shame encourage addicts to be alone, where they can drink or use without being judged. They lose interest in activities that once brought them pleasure (remember the dopamine bar?) and avoid getting together with friends and family. If they do engage with loved ones, it is often heated or uncomfortable, as the loved ones are more and more aware of the problem. If the addict is working, performance on the job suffers. And financially, addicts may be heading toward ruin, spending more time drinking or trying to buy pills, forgetting to pay the mortgage, or no longer caring how much of their retirement income they spend on their drug of choice.

As devastating as the social and emotional consequences can be, the spiritual consequences are perhaps the worst. An older adult alcoholic or addict who once placed much importance on spirituality may lose faith, thinking, perhaps, that everyone would be better off without him. This sense of not belonging is pivotal to addiction's success: At this point, addicts are obsessed with their drug of choice, the only thing that gives them a sense of relief, at least at first. As the dopamine bar rises, so does the need to consume more drugs. And then more. The addict chases the high only to be let down again and again. That first drink that calms the nerves is followed by countless more that do nothing but leave the addict in a stupor.

What Addiction Looks Like

To give you a better idea of how addiction might look in an older adult, I'm going to refer to the latest *Diagnostic and Statistical Manual of Mental Disorders* published by the American Psychiatric Association, *DSM-5*, which lists eleven criteria for substance use disorder and provides examples of the behavior associated with each criterion. Depending on how many criteria a person meets, he or she may be diagnosed with a mild, moderate, or severe substance use disorder. Here are the symptoms to look out for, based on the eleven criteria:

1. Taking a substance in larger amounts or for longer than you're meant to. After two or three refills of a mood-altering medication, the health issue should be addressed with patient and physician. Be forthright and honest about your concerns. Remember, we're particularly interested in medicines used for sleep, anxiety, stimulation, and pain.
2. Wanting to cut down or stop the substance but being unable to. Patients might say, "This drug makes me too tired. I can't function. I want to sit on the couch all the time," but when they try to decrease dosage, they report things like, "I just couldn't. My pain was too great. My anxiety was too great. I didn't sleep for three days, so I had to start my medication again." Or they might say, "I'm not going to smoke any more marijuana; it makes me paranoid," but a week later, they've bought another couple of ounces.

3. Spending a lot of time getting, using, and recovering from the substance. A patient might have two or three doctors, and call the doctor's office or the pharmacy all the time. She might feel groggy, trying to recover from medication taken the night before, and be unable to participate in important activities.
4. Having cravings and urges to use the substance. An addicted patient will say, "I need it, and I need it now—not one minute later than I'm supposed to get it." Worse, the patient might take the medication an hour or two before it's supposed to be used or might double up on the dose.
5. Not managing at work, home, or school. This behavior might include missing meals, neglecting housework and schoolwork, periods of absence from a job or school, and poor hygiene.
6. Continuing to use, even when it causes problems in a relationship. A patient will continue to use, despite the concerns of a family member. This situation creates havoc. The patient might say, "Stay out of my life. Leave me alone. It's none of your business. My doctor prescribed them for me, and that's good enough for me."
7. Giving up important social, occupational, and recreational activities. The patient might miss a grandchild's recital or a family dinner. If there's a picnic, he might decline, saying, "I can't walk on that kind of a surface." When invited to a high school basketball game, the patient might respond, "The bleachers are too uncomfortable for me. I'd rather stay home."
8. Using substances again and again, even when it puts the patient in danger. Such behavior might include falling down,

driving while intoxicated, falling asleep with the stove on, leaving the iron on, falling asleep on a couch and waking up with a backache or stiff neck, stumbling, and speaking with garbled and slurred speech.

9. Continuing to use even when the substance is causing or exacerbating a physical or psychological problem. Constipation is a huge side effect with opioids. Constipation can lead to significant bowel problems, including rupture in the colon. With antianxiety and sleeping meds, classic side effects are anxiety, angry outbursts, sleepiness, oversleeping, and lethargy.
10. Needing more of a substance to feel an effect, referred to as tolerance. Tolerance is common in patients with chronic pain. When they require more medication, a physician might double the dose. Beware when a prescription says, "Take one or two every four to six hours," and the patient takes two every four hours. The patient is opting for the higher dose. Or what used to be a glass of wine at dinner turns into half the bottle each night before bed. These should be clear signs that tolerance is developing and danger is imminent.
11. Developing withdrawal symptoms that can be relieved by taking more of the substance. These symptoms include sweating, chills, anger, anxiety, and muscle aches. If a patient says, "As soon as I wake up in the morning I take my medication," that's classic. A short-acting drug taken at nine in the evening can wear off by four in the morning. The patient then wakes up with pain and anxiety. If the medication is prescribed for ten in the morning and the patient takes it at five, six, or seven, that's a sign of a real problem.

Gone are the days when drunks were chastised as being weak, morally corrupt, and downright untreatable. Scientific data based on more than fifty years of research prove that addiction is not based on moral failure but is a chronic organic disease of the brain, affecting its structure and function. Like diabetes or hypertension, this disease requires a lifelong commitment to its management and containment. The disease is cunning, baffling, powerful, and often fatal. It can only be treated and cannot be cured.

Taking drugs or alcohol for the first time is almost always a choice or, in the case of prescription drugs, a solution. Addiction, however, is not a choice but a disease. Understanding the disease concept is critically important to the addict or alcoholic and the family. A weight is lifted, as if the shame suddenly dissipates. We must defuse the stigma, allow the treatment to begin, and help older adults find the strength and willingness to take the first steps toward recovery.

■

CHAPTER 6

Finding Help: The Older Adult and Treatment

Eleanor, age seventy-four, was a therapeutic dilemma. She had not one but three pain management specialists, as well as a cardiologist, rheumatologist, gynecological oncologist, dermatologist, and psychologist. On paper, it was clear that she was quite addicted to her pain medications, namely OxyContin, hydrocodone, and long-acting morphine sulfate, all of which she had been taking for twelve years, primarily for the pain associated with her arthritis and cancer. Her family physician also treated her for anxiety with Xanax. The drug combinations left her in a stupor, confused and amnesic, and often drifting in and out of various states and levels of consciousness. Her family members were more than concerned. Eleanor was well cared for in a senior center, but her family was beginning to connect the dots regarding Eleanor's mental state and her drug use. Even with her rheumatoid arthritis, Eleanor had always been a spry and lively personality. Maybe her confusion was not age related but drug induced? Her family sought help. Three alcohol and drug treatment centers refused admission. They were not equipped to handle Eleanor's medical and pain management issues.

Family members decided to zero in on what they needed from a treatment center. With the help of Eleanor's doctors, they did an audit of her medications and needs and came up with three major requirements: First, Eleanor would need a highly qualified team of addiction specialists who were willing to work with multiple other specialists while she attended treatment. Second, the program had to allow for very flexible treatment program scheduling. Third, the center had to be willing to meet her at her level of consciousness and mild cognitive impairment. In the beginning, at least, Eleanor would be spending more time medically detoxifying than reading assignments from her addiction counselor. When teased apart and spelled out, Eleanor's needs did not look quite so onerous—family members knew what they needed from a treatment program, and any treatment provider they approached would know whether they could handle Eleanor's case.

The family targeted centers with medical facilities on-site, an effective pain management program, and experience treating older adults. They ended up at the Betty Ford Center, where Eleanor spent four months in treatment, carefully undergoing a medically supervised detoxification, learning new pain management skills, and once the fog had cleared, comprehending addiction and recovery principles. Now she actively attends senior exercise classes, enjoys her grandchildren, and volunteers at the senior center where she was once a patient, sitting in her wheelchair in the corner, asleep. Eleanor got her life back at a time when she and her family thought it was over.

■

Age does not have to be a factor when it comes to treatment. I've seen people in their nineties recover, their world expanding to include travel and grandchildren. As the saying goes, it's never too late.

Although some people recover from alcohol or other drug addiction just by attending Alcoholics Anonymous (AA) or Narcotics Anonymous (NA) meetings or by "white knuckling" it, most people—including older adults—benefit from attending a structured treatment program that meets their unique needs. Older adults not only benefit from the experience but also usually come to relish it. But not every treatment center is prepared to handle the sometimes complicated needs of some older adults. This chapter will help you determine any special needs the older adult in your life requires from a treatment center, given his or her level of health and personal issues, and then guide you in selecting the best facility.

Knowing where, or having a good idea of where, to go for treatment before you approach your older adult about your concern is crucial. You will want to be prepared, and a big piece of your prep work involves finding a treatment center, preferably one that caters to older adults. Doing this legwork in advance is important because once you've gotten up the nerve to approach your parent or patient and he or she hesitantly agrees to concede to your wishes, you want to be able to say, "Great. Here's where we're going. Here's your bag. Here's our plane tickets (if traveling long distance). They are expecting us—let's go." There's no greater momentum killer than lack of preparation. The less time Mom has to mull over the decision, the better.

Older Adults Have Unique Treatment Needs

Ask any interventionist—a professional trained to help loved ones confront the addict with the consequences of their addiction and get them help—and you'll quickly learn that everyone under the sun can come up with endless reasons for why they can't attend a treatment program. An older adult's list of objections is likely to be not only long but also pretty reasonable, at least at first. This is because older adults have a slew of unique needs that require accommodation. Health conditions, doctor appointments, caregiving roles, transportation issues, fatigue, and other concerns common to older adults can easily interfere with a traditional treatment program's schedule, making it seemingly impossible for them to follow a treatment program, whether outpatient or residential. But overcoming these obstacles is possible. It requires some creativity on the part of caregivers, as well as a treatment program that is flexible and, ideally, either designed especially for the older adult or highly attuned to the older adult population.

Before you approach a treatment center, you will want to make sure you've taken your older adult's unique needs and potential objections into consideration. If you don't live with or care for your addicted loved one and have been out of touch with his or her day-to-day activities and overall capabilities, you might not fully grasp what the obstacles to attending treatment truly are. Let's look at some of the unique needs of this age group. Before seeking treatment options, you will want to fully understand what circumstances you need to bring to the center's attention and then be the judge of whether that center is right for your loved one.

General Health and Doctor Appointments

Unless your loved one is fit as a fiddle or falls in the younger age bracket of older adults, he or she likely has some health issues that need persistent and ongoing care. As many as 92 percent of U.S. adults age sixty-five and older have at least one chronic condition; 41 percent have three or more.[35] Chronic conditions range from high blood pressure to chronic obstructive pulmonary disease (COPD) to diabetes to kidney failure. Upcoming surgeries and periodic testing and procedures, such as colonoscopies and stress tests, are also considerations.

If your addicted parent is scheduled for surgery, relies on making regular dialysis appointments, or is being treated for cancer or another serious disease, he or she may need to be able to make it to multiple doctor appointments every month. Getting to even occasional doctor appointments is crucial for older adults, especially if they are being monitored or receiving follow-up care.

Postponing addiction treatment because of health reasons makes sense in some circumstances, but you must prioritize. Remember that addiction itself is a fatal disease. In addition, alcohol and illicit as well as prescription drugs can create or exacerbate certain health problems, such as high blood pressure and even diabetes, and create a state of confusion (as in Eleanor's case). It's highly possible that once your parent is in recovery from addiction, some of his or her health issues will disappear or diminish.

You don't have to make the decision by yourself about whether your parent or loved one is healthy enough to attend treatment. Talk to his or her doctors. In my experience, primary care doctors and specialists are extremely cooperative in helping to make addiction treatment a priority for their patients. This is a cooperative effort. And these days, treatment centers are wide open to the idea of working with a team of providers, which can include family physicians, specialists, psychologists, psychiatrists, and others. A reputable treatment facility will welcome the opportunity to collaborate with family health care providers. Your loved one's doctors should be part of the addiction treatment team.

Overall, the rule of thumb is to ensure that a treatment program can work with and around the older adult's health issues and general health care. The center you're interviewing should readily want to know what type of health care needs someone might have while in the center's care. It should have a designated health care coordinator who takes into account all medical needs and incorporates them into a treatment program in a timely fashion, making appropriate changes in level of care as necessary. The coordinator, along with the rest of the treatment team, should assess and reassess patients and, when necessary, postpone treatment in favor of treating other more pressing health concerns.

THE CHRONIC PAIN AND ADDICTION CONUNDRUM

Addiction treatment may not always be physically comfortable, but it shouldn't be physically painful either. Chronic pain is an issue for many older adults during addiction treatment. Many have been taking highly addictive and mood-altering painkillers to ease their symptoms for years. Yet the most effective addiction treatment requires that patients be abstinent of all mood-altering substances during treatment and beyond. So how do you deal with this conundrum?

Counselors are well aware that they are not going to get anywhere with a patient who is drug-free but in deep physical pain. And, of course, no one wants to see their parents suffer—to take them off painkillers, put them into addiction treatment, and trade one affliction for another. If your parent suffers from chronic pain, you will want to reach out to treatment centers that have special programs for chronic pain management during (and after) treatment. These special tracks have been created to help the burgeoning number of people who have become addicted to painkillers yet still need to address chronic pain. These types of programs consider safe, alternative methods of addressing pain as well as ways to safely monitor painkiller intake when absolutely necessary.

Caregiving Roles

Does your addicted parent care for your other parent or someone else? If so, you will want to know how involved your parent's caregiving role is. According to a 2009 national survey by the National Alliance for Caregiving and AARP, the average age of caregivers in the United States is slowly increasing, from 46.4 in 2004 to 49.2 in 2009. About 49 percent of caregivers are over age fifty, and 25 percent of older adults care for another older adult. Older adults may take care of one or more people, usually a spouse or partner but sometimes a neighbor, friend, parent, or other relative, including grandchildren.[36] According to a report by Johns

Hopkins University, the older the caregiver, the more hours he or she spends caregiving—approximately thirty to thirty-five hours a week for caregivers age sixty-five and older, which is equivalent to a full-time job.[37]

Caregivers spend a good portion of their time shopping, preparing food, doing laundry, keeping house, providing transportation, and administering medication. Many attend to personal hygiene, changing clothes and diapers, and bathing their loved one. According to AARP's Home Alone study, more and more caregivers are taking on the challenge of performing nursing tasks, such as administering medications, monitoring blood sugar and blood pressure, changing dressings, and performing physical therapy.[38] Caregiving tends to be a rewarding but overwhelming and thankless job, and caregiving for family members is usually unpaid. Finding another caregiver is difficult at best. What happens to those being cared for when the caregiver needs to spend those thirty to thirty-five caregiving hours each week in treatment? It's important to know your parent's caregiving schedule, if applicable, and to ask a prospective center what it can do to help you manage the situation.

A good adult treatment center will know the rules of the road—social service agencies and Medicare and Medicaid programs may help cover the caregiving role of an addicted older adult if this role precludes his or her participation in treatment. Qualified staff members at treatment centers know how to take the excuses away and eliminate treatment roadblocks.

Fatigue

Fatigue is common among older adults, and the reasons for it vary. As we age, our sleep patterns tend to change. Older adults spend more time in the lighter stages of sleep and wake up easily and often during the night. Interrupted sleep—and fatigue itself—can also be caused by underlying health and mental health issues as well as medications. Sleep disturbances and fatigue may also be side effects from a medication the patient may be abusing or dependent on, including alcohol. Tolerance of and withdrawal from short-acting medications, especially benzodiazepines, such as Xanax and Ativan, or sleep-inducing drugs, such as Ambien, Lunesta, and Sonata, can cause interrupted sleep and fatigue as well. Whatever the cause, the bottom line is that older adults may need long breaks and naps to help them focus and rejuvenate, and should not be expected to sit through hours of group therapy, lectures, and individual counseling before heading back to their rooms to study their assignments.

You will want to know the older adult's sleep habits when talking to a treatment center. And you'll want to know how the center deals with fatigue in its patients. Although a patient's sleep patterns need to fit into the treatment center's schedule, your loved one might require a center that allows ample time for rest and naps. In addition, a good center incorporates relaxation techniques that can take the place of a nap in the daily program. Movement classes such as Qi Gong and Tai Chi, meditation, and music therapy are a few examples. Even if the center provides designated rest and break times, know that older adults will most likely need to adjust some sleep habits. On another note, once your loved one abstains from using alcohol or other drugs, you may be surprised at how his or her sleep habits improve.

Transportation

Getting to and from treatment can be a monumental issue if the older adult doesn't have a car, is physically unable to drive, has lost the privilege to drive, or is becoming more and more fearful to drive in heavy traffic or long distances. Mom or Dad may no longer have a driver's license or a vehicle. The bus line may be inconvenient or nonexistent, and taxis might be cost prohibitive. If the older adult you care for will require transportation to and from the center, be prepared to discuss transportation issues with the treatment center. Some treatment programs will provide transportation for intensive outpatient day programs. These are typically four-hour programs, four days per week, as distinguished from residential programs where people live in the treatment center during treatment.

Addiction counselors do not typically make house calls. How your loved one gets to treatment will depend in part on his or her driving ability, who is available to help provide rides, the quality of local public transportation, whether the older adult attends residential or outpatient treatment, and whether the treatment center itself offers transport. When inquiring about transportation, you may not know the level of care the older adult requires, so be sure to ask about schedules and transportation options for all levels of care (outpatient and residential). Most people do find a way to get to treatment.

OUTPATIENT VERSUS RESIDENTIAL TREATMENT

Every patient who enters treatment has a common denominator: addiction. Otherwise, each is somewhat unique, and that's why treatment centers evaluate patients before admitting them to treatment. An evaluation helps clinicians determine the level of care a patient needs. The two major levels are outpatient and residential. Which one your loved one is placed in depends on a number of factors, including degree of dependence, whether he or she has been in treatment before, and in the case of older adults, personal schedule, health conditions, and transportation issues.

In outpatient treatment, patients usually travel three to four days a week to their program at the treatment facility. These programs may run from 9:00 a.m. to 1:00 p.m., 1:00 p.m. to 5:00 p.m., or 5:00 p.m. to 9:00 p.m., depending on the size of the facility and the number of people it serves. Outpatient programs typically last eight to twelve weeks. Patients sleep in their own home, and family members usually attend one session every week or two. Outpatient programs are ideal for the less-severe cases of addiction and are less expensive.

Residential programs vary from thirty to ninety-plus days and provide all meals and lodging for the patient in a therapeutic community. Treatment days may be six to eight hours long, five to six days a week. These are ideal for the more severely addicted patients, patients with co-occurring mental health disorders, and patients who relapse after an intensive outpatient treatment or residential care.

In general, residential is more intensive than outpatient, but for some it is less stressful as they are not in their usual environment, where they may be tempted to drink or take drugs, especially in early recovery when cravings are powerful.

The best course of action is to begin with a thorough diagnostic and clinical evaluation, including a history and physical exam; psychological, psychometric, and psychiatric testing; and a careful evaluation of reports from family, the workplace, legal authorities, and others. This information will inform clinicians regarding the proper level of care for your mom or dad.

Dementia and Other Mental Health Issues

As you learned in chapter 3 (and in the case of Eleanor), it's possible that Mom's dementia is substance induced rather than age induced. Physicians and family members alike will often mistake psychiatric symptoms for dementia or a mood, anxiety, or sleep disorder but, in addiction, psychiatric symptoms can be the result of using alcohol or other drugs. The only way to know for sure is for an older adult to become clean and sober. Once the mind and body have had an opportunity to heal, if the dementia or other mental health issues still exist, the older adult will need clinicians trained to deal with co-occurring disorders—the combination of one or more mental health issues and addiction.

For people of all ages who enter treatment, a diagnosis of co-occurring disorders has become the norm. Most addicted patients suffer from depression, anxiety, or another mental health issue and may need medications to treat the more severe disorders. Depression is a common co-occurring disorder that may require antidepressants, either for the short or long term. These medications are not addictive and may be used after discharge but must be evaluated for their interaction with other medications that your loved one may require. Because it is difficult to determine what came first—the mental health issue or the alcohol/drug dependence—more and more centers have clinicians who are trained to treat both at the same time. Evaluations, detoxification, and abstinence followed by ongoing evaluations help clinicians understand the effect of substance use on mental health and brain disorders, and vice versa. Once clinicians know what they are dealing with, they can intervene with the appropriate medical care if necessary. To get a valid evaluation of cognitive function, it is imperative to get the patient drug- and alcohol-free. Periodic reexamination of memory and speed of processing data, multitasking, and decision-making ability helps determine whether the thought disturbance is primary and independent, or whether it is drug induced.

If Mom or Dad's dementia is far enough along that you fear she or he will not benefit from treatment, you will want to discuss your concern with your parent's physician. This is where the services of a geriatric psychiatrist and/or neurologist come into play, using the services of memory disorder clinics and psychological testing, if possible, with one-on-one interviews. These specialists can evaluate the dementia and determine a person's ability to participate in treatment. They can also define special needs—perhaps more one-on-one time, more conjoint therapy work (where multiple family members are seen together), and more elaborate support from the family post-treatment.

If possible, take the older adult you care for to a geriatric psychiatrist trained in addiction medicine. Most doctors receive little training in addiction medicine, and some are misinformed about what it takes to recover from the disease.

Finances

Finances can be a sticky issue, especially for older adults who are saving for retirement, retired and living on a limited income, or retired and unable to return to work. Stress over finances may have contributed to the reason your parent started to drink or use drugs to excess in the first place. No one dreams of shelling out thousands of dollars to pay for addiction treatment, and parting with the funds—especially in retirement—can be painful for the addicted adult and everyone concerned. On the other hand, not having funds does not mean that an older adult can't receive treatment. Insurance and patient aid are options you will want to explore. The Affordable Care Act (ACA) is providing more comprehensive insurance for outpatient addiction treatment, and most treatment centers can assist with the preapproval process.

"Buyer beware": The ACA has spawned a slew of upstart outpatient programs. Look for a certified outpatient program with experience treating older adults, one with the sensitivity and capability to employ counselors with specific skills in treating this population. Not just any outpatient program will do. Some are very skilled. Gather information about the center's population by asking specific questions: How many older adults (age fifty-five to sixty-five; age sixty-five and older) are under your care? What is the average age of patients? How old is your oldest patient? May I come in and observe a group or two to see whether the program fits us?

QUESTIONS TO ASK YOURSELF WHEN CONSIDERING TREATMENT

- What, if any, health or mental health conditions does Dad suffer from?
- What medications does he take?
- Is it possible a medical condition has gone undiagnosed?
- How often does he need to go to the doctor or other essential appointments?
- Does Dad suffer from fatigue?
- How much sleep does he get?
- What are his sleep patterns?
- Does he take naps?
- For whom is Dad responsible?
- Who would need help if Dad went to treatment?
- What are his caregiving duties?
- How much time does he spend caregiving?
- Can he drive to treatment, or does he need to be in a residential setting?
- Who can help with transportation?
- What is Dad's financial situation?
- How much can we spend on addiction treatment services?
- Will insurance cover any of the cost?
- Does Dad qualify for financial aid at any treatment center?

What to Look for in an Older Adult Treatment Program

Historically, treatment for addiction to alcohol and other drugs has been divided by age (youths, young adults, and adults), as well as by gender. The Hanley Center in Florida was the first treatment center to address the needs of the older adult. Since it opened in 1955, only a handful of centers have followed suit. Even with the large numbers of older adults needing help, the market has been slow to respond, although more and more centers are offering specific tracks for older adults, just as they might for lawyers, health care professionals, LGBTQ people, or people suffering from both an eating disorder and alcohol or other drug addiction. These days, treatment for older adults comes in three basic forms: centers devoted to treating older adults (sometimes divided by age group: ages forty-six to sixty-four and ages sixty-five and older); centers that treat adults and have special programming for older adults; and centers that treat older adults along with other adults and do not offer any special programming. All of them can work (and have worked for years for thousands of people), but you will want to consider the level of older adult involvement that's right for your loved one.

Most older adults enjoy the company of any age group, but many prefer to go through treatment with their peers. Generally, twenty-two-year-olds face different issues and are far less mature in how they describe and cope with their issues than are seventy-year-olds. Most older adults in treatment are more interested in camaraderie than confrontation and may feel uncomfortable or even ashamed being vulnerable in front of a young adult. If the older adult does not identify with the younger adult (and vice versa), it becomes an easy out. "I can't be addicted. I haven't spent time in jail or done hard drugs like crystal meth."

Adolescents and young adults (up to age twenty-six) are typically treated with their peers because it's easier for youths to be honest and forthright among those with whom they identify. This honesty and opening up, so crucial to the recovery process, is best achieved among peers. The same applies to older adults. Their thoughts and beliefs about addiction and recovery may be miles apart from those even twenty years younger than they are. Among their peers, older adults are more likely to find communion and fellowship, ripening the environment for spiritual bonds that feed the recovery of each individual in the group.

Likewise, gender-specific programming is important regardless of age. The desire for love and affection can be alive at any age, and during treatment and early recovery, this desire is a major distraction. Although men and women may mingle during social activities and free time, they are best kept separate in therapy sessions so that they can focus on their recovery rather than the affections of another. Separating the sexes also allows men and women to feel safe disclosing personal stories and insights that may be specific to their gender.

Finding the most appropriate treatment facility for the older adult can feel like a challenge, but if you know what to look for, suddenly the task is not so daunting. Now that you have thought through some of your parent's unique needs and considered the two basic levels of programming (inpatient and outpatient), it's a lot easier to know what to ask about and expect from a facility. In general, whether in outpatient or residential treatment, older adults benefit from the following:

- a qualified treatment team (with on-site medical facility for medically compromised patients)
- a flexible schedule (freedom to leave for caregiving duties or doctor appointments)
- long, scheduled breaks to rest or nap
- extended periods for socializing with other older adults
- group meetings and activities with other older adults

- communicative staff members who take an interest in helping you and your parent resolve issues related to treatment
- a case management program

Qualified Treatment Team

Most addiction counselors and other staff are passionate about their work. Many, if not most, are in recovery themselves. But it's important for you to have a strong sense of how qualified they are. Clinicians can have various and multiple certifications and degrees—LAC, LACD, CACD (I, II, III), RN, MSW, PsyD, MD, and the list goes on and on. Ask the center who will be involved in your loved one's caregiving. A comprehensive team usually includes a licensed or certified addiction counselor, psychiatrist or psychologist, social worker, nutritionist, spiritual counselor, and wellness coach. All medical staff should be trained in addiction, and someone on the team should be qualified to address co-occurring disorders. It's also imperative that the treatment team seek out and include the older adult's current health care providers when developing a treatment plan, on and off during treatment, and when determining a continuing care plan.

A Flexible Schedule

Treatment centers that serve younger populations tend to be structured and rule oriented. Patients are expected to be on time for group and appointments, to stay on campus unless on a family pass with permission, and to be in their rooms by curfew. Rules and structure promote self-discipline, which encourages the development of integrity, honesty, and many of the other principles inherent in the Twelve Step program of recovery, which is a part of most treatment programs. In older adult settings, patients still benefit from structure and rules, but providers for older adults bend them to ensure the older adult can stick with treatment. It does little good to insist a patient miss a dialysis appointment in order to attend group. Some centers will design a treatment plan around an individual's work, volunteer, or caregiving responsibilities with the understanding that most older adults will recover but, typically, at a slower pace than their younger counterparts.

Long Breaks

Treatment is not meant to be a vacation, but older adults require extended breaks for several reasons. First, addiction takes a huge toll on a person physically, mentally, and spiritually. In recovery, the body, mind, and spirit begin the healing process. Healing takes energy. On top of it all, older adults may feel uncomfortable being out of their normal setting; worry about finances, a spouse, family, or a pet; or have coexisting physical or mental health issues. At the end of the day, the patient is exhausted and unable to absorb pertinent recovery information.

Treatment is not designed to wear a person down. Treatment is designed to uplift and rejuvenate. The simple fact is that older adults need adequate time to rest during the day, and some need more than others. Older adults do better when breaks for rests and naps are built into the treatment schedule.

Extended Periods for Socializing with Other Older Adults

Older adults who enjoy the community aspect of recovery—the Twelve Step meetings, fellowship, and recovery-specific events and activities—tend to flourish in recovery. Isolation can be a fact of life for many older adults, although it's not always by choice. Feeling that we belong to a community is life giving, a basic human need. Recovery communities across the nation are often vibrant and active, and some communities schedule events specifically for older adults in recovery. During treatment, when patients open up to each other and find that their feelings, thoughts, beliefs, and experiences around addiction are similar to others in their group, a new world opens up to them. This connection can bring joy and peace and the feeling that life is full again.

Case Management

Case managers work with the older adult before, during, and after treatment. They are a single "go-to" person for you and the older adult when it comes to referrals, social services, compliancy (with a licensing board, for instance, if your loved one is a working doctor, lawyer, or other licensed professional), and general advocacy. Case managers possess a wealth of information and can connect you and your parent with needed resources. They can make your life a lot easier by pointing you in the right direction.

QUESTIONS TO ASK PROVIDERS:

- Is your treatment program geared toward older adults?
- Is the program age- and gender-specific?
- Do you have a medical doctor on staff?
- How often do patients see the doctor?
- What steps do you take to communicate with a patient's health care providers outside of treatment?
- How do you handle dementia?
- Are your clinicians trained to treat co-occurring disorders?
- Are health care providers considered part of the treatment team?
- My mom has difficulty (fill in the blank). Do you make any allowances to help her treat her condition? (Add your own list of conditions.)
- What is a typical day of treatment like for older adults?

- What type of evaluation do you do?
- What if my older adult has caregiving duties?
- Do you offer transportation services?
- How much can we expect to spend on treatment?
- What insurance do you accept?
- Do you offer financial aid?
- Do you have case managers?
- May I observe a day in treatment to see whether it feels right for my loved one?

Specify your loved one's needs. Separate them out so you can tackle them one step at a time. Be honest with any treatment center you talk to. Hide none of these needs. The right treatment center can and will accommodate you and your loved one.

Making the Transition

When it comes to the point where we need to do something we don't want to do, the immediate reaction is to rattle off a litany of excuses forty layers deep. This is usually because, deep down, we're afraid of change, failure, or even success. As adult children, we might fear leaving our vulnerable parent in a strange place with clinicians who follow some clinically and spiritually based process we know little about to somehow, miraculously, get our parent clean and sober. The addicted older adult may be far more reluctant. But now is not the time to cave in to anyone's fears. Treatment doesn't have to be a mystery or something to fear. Find out as much as you can about how the treatment center will meet your loved one's very specific needs. The more information you have, the more you will feel assured that the older adult can not only make it to, but also is even likely to enjoy, treatment, and the more comfortable you will feel.

Everyone has to make hard decisions at some point in life. Call upon your inner strength, and listen to those who have gone before you. Millions of others have walked this same path, made this same difficult transition, and come out happier and healthier despite the odds. You and your loved one have nothing to lose and everything to gain.

■

CHAPTER 7

Getting an Older Adult to Accept Help

Robert, in his early sixties, was widowed five years ago when his wife died in a car accident. He held a job in a car factory for more than thirty years, and he and his wife had raised three children, now grown and doing well. The kids were close to their dad, even more so after their mom's passing. It was normal for Robert to drink a beer or two at night and at football games, but addiction had never been an issue in the family. At age sixty-two, Robert suffered a mild stroke, from which he recovered easily. He did decide, however, to take an early retirement. After his stroke, he worried about being frail and not being able to be as active with his family. Depressed and living alone in isolation, he started drinking more.

At a follow-up appointment with his doctor, Robert complained that he was having trouble sleeping. His doctor gave him something for his sleepless nights and something for his anxiety. Upon filling the prescriptions, the pharmacist instructed Robert not to use alcohol while under the influence of these new drugs. Robert started taking his new prescription drugs as directed, but he did not stop drinking. After about six months on his regimen of pills and beer, he stumbled around the house, fell down, and cut his head. His son found him and took him to the emergency room. The ER doctor expressed some concern about the toxic combination of medications and alcohol, but Robert denied knowing that he couldn't mix the two. Robert's son wasn't so sure. He had suspected for some time that his dad wasn't visiting as often because he didn't want to show up intoxicated.

The family opted to do an informal intervention of their own. They each wrote letters expressing how much Robert meant to them and how they were feeling the negative impact of his drinking. At the intervention, they read them aloud: One grandchild said he missed playing chess on Thursday nights, a daughter said she felt let down that Robert never showed up to help fix her car when promised, and his son missed watching football games together. No one pointed fingers at Robert. The intervention was an opportunity to show him how much love they had for him. Robert agreed to go to a day treatment program, where he learned about the disease, learned about his medical condition, got together with other adults, and realized he was lucky that his stroke was mild. Today Robert enjoys an active recovery, sees his grandchildren, doesn't drink alcohol, takes medications only as directed by the doctor, and drinks herbal tea to help him sleep.

■

You've done your homework and found one or more treatment centers for your loved one. Now you need to get your addicted older adult through the door. In most cases of addiction, bringing up the subject of treatment is touchy. You can expect to confront anything from complete acceptance to flat-out denial that a problem exists. Most people fall somewhere in-between: They may know they have a problem, they aren't happy with how life is going, but they don't want to change.

Your biggest hurdle in getting your loved one to treatment is not logistical or financial. Instead, be prepared for what many older adults hold on to for dear life: denial and independence.

Denial Is Not a River in Egypt

Alcoholics and addicts who are in recovery joke about denial. They see how this powerful psychological defense blinds us from seeing anything resembling the truth.

Denial stems from our beliefs, usually some hard-core beliefs. If we suspect something is happening that is contrary to those beliefs, we pull out our toolbox of coping mechanisms. Denial, the most convenient of our tools, is at the ready when we need it. We get into a state of denial when the truth is too hard for us to bear—when the truth doesn't fit our image of ourselves.

Denial has many faces. We might deny that we have terminal cancer, because we don't see ourselves as dying. We might deny that our spouse is cheating, because we can't imagine living without this person or being divorced. We might spend money foolishly, because to admit that we are broke is too painful. If a loved one is in denial about alcohol or drug abuse, getting him or her to face reality is extremely difficult. No matter what you say, an addict is likely to deny the facts—and even blame you and others. The idea of living without the drug of choice is unbearable, like losing a best friend or an important source of support.

Not all addicts are in denial about their use, at least to themselves. Many people understand that they have a problem, to one degree or another, even if they won't admit to it. Some people despise their dependence on a drug and what has happened to them because of it. Still, denial will usually cloud an addict's self-perception, and you can expect persistent resistance to treatment or any move that appears to threaten their drug use.

Denial and the Older Adult

Denial of addiction is stronger in older adults than it is in young people. The reasons why may be unique to those who formed an opinion about alcoholics and drug addicts before the 1950s.

The 1950s saw a marked change in how Americans viewed drinking. For many, it was fashionable, a sign of post–World War II prosperity, to have a cocktail before dinner, wine with a meal, and after-dinner drinks. Not all families behaved this way, but alcohol advertising campaigns made cocktail hour look appealing. The people in the ads were happy—smiling and laughing with a group of people—not stumbling down a dark alley alone. Alcohol use became synonymous with fun and success. Before then, excessive drinking was viewed not as a show of prosperity but as a moral failing. In the 1950s, it was seen as a moral failing if you weren't able to control your drinking and meet the community standards of success and propriety. The value this generation placed on morality was high, and the moral compass always pointed in the same direction. Right and wrong was black and white, not as gray as it tends to be today. It would be decades before alcoholism and addiction to other drugs would start to be accepted by the general public as a disease instead of a moral failing to be denied, hidden, or punished. For people whose attitudes were shaped during the 1950s, this acceptance has been even slower in coming.

Ingrained beliefs do not die easily. When it comes to addiction, most older adults do not want to be seen as moral failures, especially if they've lived with integrity. Failing morally has spiritual and community repercussions, including the threat of being treated as an outcast and, for some religious people, of going to hell. Frightened and ashamed, many older adults who suffer from addiction turn to denial to save their self-image.

Perhaps the older man, once the patriarch who responsibly

cared for his family, cannot face that he has let his family down. Or the mother who raised her children with love and acceptance, and who is now slurring her words, is too embarrassed to spend time with her grandchildren. Rather than understanding that they have a disease that needs to be treated, these older adults believe they have failed on every front. Stigma and shame combine to encourage isolation. Typically, the more severe a person's addiction, the stronger the denial and desperation to protect the ability to drink or use.

The shame that fuels denial is a universal human emotion. Even younger generations, who have been exposed to the disease concept, still experience shame and denial, but they often have more open-mindedness. They may have learned about addictive family systems in health or psychology classes in high school or college. They are more likely to know people who are open about being in recovery, and they may be familiar with books, television shows, or movies that explore the nature of addiction and recovery.

Denial Flows Both Ways

Addicts and alcoholics aren't the only people who experience denial. Family members and caregivers also can find it hard to admit that a loved one is addicted. Since you are reading this book, your denial is probably starting to crumble. Others, however, may still firmly deny that Mom, Dad, or Grandma has a drinking or drug problem. If addiction is clearly the issue, it helps to have everyone united in helping that loved one get sober.

The Bootstrap Syndrome

> "Freedom (n.): To ask nothing. To expect nothing. To depend on nothing."
>
> —AYN RAND, *THE FOUNTAINHEAD*

The idea of freedom is valued very highly by most people, especially in America. For most of us, freedom means we have a sense of independence to live as we please. Independence is a concept that many older adults cling to as if it were life itself. Gradually, as we age, we lose what may have been sources of pride for us—beauty, power, and strength. Knee replacements leave us unable to ski, arthritis limits our ability to crochet, and poor eyesight forces us to forfeit our driver's license. With each loss comes a sense of grief. We don't like to see ourselves as helpless, and we don't want to depend on others. In our stubbornness to keep our independence—our freedom—we refuse help, insisting we don't need to go to assisted living or have a personal aide. Giving up independence is giving up life as we know it.

This fear of losing independence is nearly universal. Admitting we can't handle everything on our own or asking for help would be considered weak. Many older people would rather be miserable than weak. They want to pick themselves up by their bootstraps, like they've done throughout life.

Most older adults don't want to see themselves as old and needy. Their spirits are as young as ever. Even as they accept certain conditions such as arthritis, they still see themselves as capable of caring for themselves.

This resistance to accepting help carries over into addiction with a vengeance. Fortunately, many tried-and-true methods exist to ease people into accepting help.

Approaching an Older Adult about Treatment

Even though you may be somewhat prepared for your loved one to resist treatment, the following approaches can help pave the path toward treatment and sobriety.

Conduct an Intervention

An intervention happens when family and friends sincerely reveal to the addict or alcoholic that his or her using behavior is out of hand. These family and friends talk about how much they care about the addict—but assert that they can no longer live with the addictive behavior. Entire books have been written and television series produced about alcohol and drug intervention. Some interventions are more dramatic than others—and some are more successful than others.

It's possible that the older adult will refuse help, yet refusal does not mean failure. By stating the issue, you've planted a seed. Regardless of the outcome, interventions are especially helpful when addicts start to realize how their addiction affects other people.

The purpose of an intervention is to concentrate family members' effort and concern; ultimately, family members are advocating for proper treatment for the alcoholic or addict. Preparing for the intervention is critical, so all family members share the same agenda of getting treatment. This is a family disease, and often a codependent family member will try to protect the alcoholic or addict from the truth. This family member might say, "Oh, he's not that bad," or "She doesn't need to go to treatment," or "You're making a mountain out of a molehill," or "Don't embarrass our mother." Sometimes that person may also have a substance use disorder and is trying to protect herself as well as the addicted loved one.

When there is dissension among family members, it may be time to find the best interventionist possible. A professional interventionist can recognize family conflicts and help avoid a catastrophic or an aborted intervention. An interventionist provides leadership and educates everyone to see that treatment is not punishment and that an intervention is not a character assassination: It is a straightforward way to recommend treatment for a fatal disease. A good interventionist will help family members keep in mind that alcoholics or addicts cannot advocate for themselves, nor can they find help without the support of others.

What If They Refuse Treatment?

If an older adult refuses treatment for severe alcoholism or other drug addiction, family members need to be aware that cognitive impairment issues may exist. Is the older adult able to advocate for himself? Should you seek a power of attorney? Is the older adult capable of making sound decisions? Older adults can be recommended to treatment by a judge. Often a judge will recommend that the older adult at least be evaluated and held for seventy-two hours of observation and evaluation. If the person continues to fight treatment, a hearing presenting the results of the evaluation may be done before an administrative judge. If a person still refuses treatment, the treatment for substance abuse may morph into treatment for mental incapacity.

In situations like this, a family's best course of action is to act together and protect the addicted individual from further harm. Be clear about avoiding codependent, enabling actions that will put that older adult at further risk. For example, refuse to take the person to buy liquor. Insist that someone lives with the older adult, whether a professional caregiver or a relative, despite steadfast claims that she wants to be alone. Be aware that the person may require an assisted living situation. This depends on the person's age, health status, and, more important, mental status. Sometimes a caring brother or sister who is the same age as the individual can be invited to stay with the person and help her calm down until the intervention can be repeated from a different angle. A trusted physician and professional interventionist working together in these cases can be very helpful.

Getting the Assessment

At a minimum, encourage your loved one to agree to take an assessment online, over the phone, or in person. If the person refuses treatment, challenge him or her to call the treatment center for a free assessment. If they don't have a problem, what have they got to lose?

Resistance is normal. No one wants to go under the microscope. Be patient and give your loved one time. Assure him or her that no commitment is involved; an assessment is just like going to any other physician. No one is going to point fingers. An assessment is a caring and loving way to see what is going on and what can be done about it. Let your loved one know that you and your family are worried. An assessment is a way to help all family members deal with their concerns. More than likely, the assessment will result in treatment options. In rare cases, further assessment is required to determine the level and nature of cognitive disability.

The best course of action is to begin with a thorough diagnostic and clinical evaluation, including a health history and physical exam; psychological, psychometric, and psychiatric testing; and a full evaluation of reports from family, the workplace, legal authorities, and others. This information will inform clinicians regarding the proper level of care for an older adult.

Transition Day

If the assessment confirms that the older adult has an addiction disorder and needs treatment, and he or she has agreed to go, it is important to make the transition from home to treatment as painless as possible. On transition day, it is always helpful to have a small group of trusted family members accompany the person to treatment. This group might include the family physician, a trusted nurse, and a close relative, such as a grown child. We had one woman come into treatment at the Betty Ford Center not long ago accompanied by twelve family members. It was a fiasco. The woman adamantly opposed treatment, stayed only three or four days, then left abruptly against medical advice. Her supporting cast of characters were long gone by that time.

What works best is to have one or two people bring the older adult to the treatment facility. This group can talk with a counselor, and the patient can tour the facility. The patient can see where he or she will sleep, talk with other patients their age, and have lunch at the facility to decide how the place feels. Two or three days later, after going home and discussing it with a physician and family, the person can return to the facility, which will then feel a bit more familiar. Hopefully, the person will be more open to trying treatment.

If an older adult isn't severely physically or mentally impaired, and isn't willing to try treatment right away—or is waiting for a bed, or simply isn't able to afford treatment—there are AA and NA meetings in every community that can provide support and a safe place to work a Twelve Step recovery program. Before treatment became more readily available, people used AA and NA, along with counseling for co-occurring disorders, as their principal recovery program. You can find groups through your friends or fellow community members, or by going to the AA or NA websites for active meetings in your area and for literature to introduce you and your loved one to their programs. Often, you can find someone from the group to take your loved one to meetings. It's important to shop around and find meetings that have the right chemistry for your loved one.

Finding a sponsor as soon as possible to help work a Twelve Step program is also important. (See the "Meetings and Membership" section of chapter 10, Staying on Track in Recovery, for more information.) Please note that neither AA nor NA is the same as treatment and doesn't provide the professional services that a treatment program offers. Twelve Step programs won't work for everyone as their principal recovery option, especially for addressing the complex needs of many older adults.

We must respect a person's initial resistance to treatment or going to AA or NA. Resistance is the nature of the disease. That doesn't mean that the patient doesn't want help. Support the person in feeling like he or she is making a worthy and right decision, and advocating for their own health. Respect the person; don't treat them like an incompetent child. Allow the person to see what is offered, meet the staff, get acquainted, and then make a reasonable decision.

■

CHAPTER 8

Every Day a Miracle

In this chapter, I give you a personal portrait of what happens in one treatment program by describing a typical day for me at the Betty Ford Center where I practice. Much of what I describe is typical of many inpatient and day programs, but there will be differences from one treatment center to the other, with greater differences found among outpatient programs.

My day starts at 4:00 a.m. I love this time of the morning. The world is quiet. The moon is still up, and I can get some work done. I start the day with some quiet prayer and meditation just to get my attitude right—gratitude for all that I have and the kind of work I'm able to do today.

I usually hit the detoxification center at the Betty Ford Center around 6:30 in the morning and start making my rounds, visiting patients who were admitted the night before or within the last couple of days. I meet with each of them to check the quality of their symptoms, evaluate mental status, and make any necessary adjustments in their treatment regimen to make them as comfortable as possible. On this particular day, I enter a room in the detox unit to find an assistant sitting with Rose, a seventy-six-year-old patient who's been with us for three days and three nights. Seeing the assistant tells me that Rose had a difficult night. In detox, patients are given drugs to ease symptoms of withdrawal and make them as comfortable as possible. But older adult patients, in addition to having to go through withdrawal, are sometimes upset by the unfamiliar surroundings in which they find themselves.

This is a familiar story for any hospitalization of an older adult. Unlike young adults, who often come in angry, resentful, and uncooperative, older adults can become frightened and disoriented. They may become combative with staff and fearful that they are losing control. Their behavior is not based on fear of what will happen, as it is with young adults, but on the more desperate fear that they don't know or understand what's happening. They might sleep poorly and scream out in the middle of the night with nightmares or wander around aimlessly in this unfamiliar territory, getting lost or falling. Bowel irregularity, fluctuations in appetite, instability of gait, memory disturbances, and mood fluctuations are common. They may be very teary or very angry, histrionic, or psychotic. These symptoms, the body lamenting the loss of its drug of choice, gradually diminish but can be scary for patients and family at first.

At the first sign of such disorientation, staff at the Betty Ford Center assign a one-on-one, 24/7 assistant to these patients. Assistants help patients to the bathroom, read at their bedside while they are sleeping, help them to the cafeteria, get their food, have comforting conversations of support, and call for a nursing assistant or physician assistance if needed.

Rose had been experiencing hallucinations and anxiety, so the assistant stayed with her to kindly and gently assure her that things would be better in the morning. And they are. Now after four days, Rose is sitting up in her bed and smiles when I greet her, a major improvement over day one. Rose had come to us on the verge of becoming addicted to painkillers and on a toxic combination of medications that caused her to hallucinate and have other dementia-like symptoms. Her husband was the first one to be concerned about her behavior. He would dispense her medication in the morning and again before bedtime. Her prescription drugs included Ambien, Valium, and Percocet. The medications she took for high blood pressure did not concern him. What bothered him most was how desperate and even angry she would become when he would give her only the prescribed dosage of Percocet, a painkiller the doctor had given Rose only a month earlier for a broken rib she had suffered from falling in the shower. She was also starting to have hallucinations, as well as forgetting who and where she was. This behavior was unlike Rose, who normally had a high tolerance for pain, rarely complained, and had been mentally intact. Rose's husband had arranged for an assessment of her drug use. Subsequently, she wound up at the Betty Ford Center to be treated for a mild substance use disorder.

Now she appears tired and still a little anxious, but her nerves are no longer on edge, the hallucinations have ceased, and she can carry on a normal conversation. This is a remarkable recovery but not uncommon.

On my rounds, I pay special attention to the medical and psychological needs of each patient. Our patients with an addiction disorder may be suffering from chronic pain, which makes it imperative that the treatment regimen be individualized. One of the first things we do upon patients' admission is audit their medication regimen. A thorough review of their drugs of choice, be it alcohol or sedatives, may predict some of their detoxification symptoms. Indeed, some of these symptoms may mimic dementia or produce psychosis with hallucinations. Withdrawal may be frightening, but it's always short-lived. Withdrawal has predictable patterns, and we've helped enough patients to know how to get both patients and family through it. Today, I assure Rose and her husband that the symptoms were worth it. What's around the corner—a life free from the harmful effects of toxic drug combinations—would be more than worth it.

I taper Rose's medication and recommend she rest. I know that her next few nights in detox will still be uneasy but much quieter. I predict she soon will be able to check in to the treatment unit, a less sterile and much homier setting where she will, like most patients, feel less threatened by her surroundings.

Satisfied that Rose and the other patients in detox are doing as well as can be expected, I move on. What happens next is always a spiritual experience for me. At about 8:00 a.m., I get to meet people on their very first day of treatment, which means I have the opportunity to make someone feel safe and comfortable and loved in our treatment setting.

Patients are often admitted before they meet with a physician. Their luggage is searched, their paperwork completed, their family educated about the process. Depending on their condition, a patient may be assigned a one-on-one assistant from the get-go. After a complete nursing evaluation, the admitting physician gives treatment orders. Usually at seven or eight the next morning, the patient meets with the physician for a complete history and physical examination. This may go very smoothly for the patient or it can be quite frightening. The job of the physician is to make patients comfortable, to assure them that they're safe, that they will be able to reach their family, and that their needs will be fulfilled. Special attention to other medical needs and the knowledge that they will be in contact with their own personal physician are also extremely comforting to the patient.

Today I meet Charlie, a sixty-eight-year-old retired electrician. Charlie's son brought him to the center, concerned that his dad's drinking had gotten way out of hand since he'd retired. Charlie lives alone. His wife of forty-three years died last year of cancer, and their four children are grown with lives of their own. Charlie is quiet and a little withdrawn, full of shame. I feel his pain, having been in that situation myself.

We establish that I will be part of his treatment team from now on and that other professionals will be supporting him as well. I let him know what to expect during detox and that I will be visiting him two or three times in his room today. Helping patients feel protected and safe before detoxification symptoms begin is paramount. As noted before, for older adults especially, detox can be traumatic at first. Charlie will be withdrawing from alcohol, which can be painful, even deadly, if not done under professional supervision and with the aid of medication. As Charlie thanks me for my help, I can feel a slight tremor in his handshake, the beginning of the delirium tremors, or the DTs. Charlie will be okay, I think. He already possesses humility in spades.

I grab a cup of coffee before heading to what we call the bed meeting, where counselors present case information on each of their patients, and, as a group of professionals, we make sure that any given patient's treatment needs are anticipated, planned for, and met. Here we assign a number for the level of care, which tells us how much observation, one-on-one assistance, nursing, monitoring, and physician attendance is needed. A frank discussion with the nursing department, with counselors, with the nutrition department, and with physicians takes place. We do our best to anticipate when the patient may begin to have more problems with detoxification, require medication assistance, need an appropriate outside referral to a hospital-based physician in a certain specialty, or be transferred to the next level of care in our residence halls, where there is less direct nurse supervision. We make it a practice to closely monitor older adult patients for five to ten days before they can move to a residence hall. Sometimes, they'll move on with their one-on-one assistant. Sometimes, they'll be in a wheelchair. Sometimes we assign them to a pain management track. We establish a fitness level to determine how much they can participate in our daily fitness program. We also pay close attention to patients' emotional needs, which sometimes center on family. The family's needs are also addressed in this multidisciplinary meeting.

The team brings up Rose. Her primary counselor suggests moving her to a treatment unit in a couple of days. I second the notion, provided she's still stable and her hallucinations have indeed ceased. She is also a candidate for our pain management track. Although her rib pain is acute, she will have it for the next month or so. In addition, she will benefit by learning remarkably effective and drug-free methods for dealing with any pain she may experience in the future.

It is absolutely a miracle to watch older adults clear from their confusion, the smiles return to their faces, to see them begin to care about other patients, to see mothers become mothers and teachers become teachers. Many older adults also turn out to be amazing mentors to their treatment peers during this period.

I particularly like treating older adults because they are so profoundly grateful when you tell them how far they've come since entering treatment. At three weeks, they often get that same kind of feedback from family members who come in and see this miraculous change. It is an absolute joy to witness the miracle of recovery. With older adults the joy is twofold, as the improvement in their health is overwhelmingly obvious. Lucidity resurfaces, blood pressure lowers, skin has a healthful glow, and their eyes are clear—it's like night and day compared to when they were admitted.

I head over to the family center, where the family members of patients who have been in the treatment program for about three weeks come and take part in a weeklong program to help them better understand addiction and how it has impacted their lives. I have the honor of being the first lecturer on Monday morning to these wonderful people, who may be feeling scared, confused, angry, or betrayed—the collateral damage of the disease of addiction. What family members learn in the program changes their lives. They see the world and their circumstances in a new light. They start to breathe again.

I finish that lecture by 11:30, grab a little lunch, and on a really good day I get to work out in our facility's wonderful gym. Several staff members are regulars, and it's always a pleasure to see people taking care of themselves in the middle of their day. But if I'm not in the gym, often this time is filled with meetings and visitors, people touring the center, or other special events.

The afternoon usually begins with another lecture. Today I will lecture our day treatment patients about denial. I throw in some interesting anecdotes about my own denial when I was drinking—and when I was in early recovery. When I am able to show my vulnerability and my humility, I am better able to reach my audience. I know when I've made a connection; I can see it in their eyes. People are hungry for healing. When they hear words that open up a new perspective, a new way of seeing themselves and their disease, they light up, even if only for a moment. That's when I know a seed has been planted and that hope does indeed spring eternal.

These folks attend treatment during the day and then return to their homes in the evening. They are usually not as severely addicted as residential patients. Some of them attend day treatment after a residential stint. They need the reinforcement, to hear the recovery message again and again until they fully understand it, and they welcome being in a safe recovery environment. At least in the beginning. In early recovery, walking past a bar or seeing a beer commercial, a medicine vial, or a needle are triggers to use. Triggers, of course, are everywhere.

Next I have an opportunity to sit down with our professional group, called the Professional Forum, made up of addicted lawyers and physicians and pilots and celebrities and businesspeople, who have a different dynamic in the development of their disease and need a different approach from a treatment perspective to break through the malignant denial. Their status and profession have enabled them to progress in their disease as family and colleagues cover up for them and make excuses for their using. After all, they have much to lose, both in status and financially, if they fall.

Big egos are in this room, and they must be dealt with and leveled in order for the patients to make some progress in this program. Many of the older adults we care for are professionals, often responsible for multiple employees and large organizations, and have a great deal of responsibility attached to their profession. Breaking through the rigid walls of these carefully protected egos is a critical part of introducing the spiritual aspect of recovery. The humility necessary for long-term recovery is vital, in this population especially. In my professionals group, I see miracles all the time. Anger, resentment, and hostility vanish. Fortunately, no one is required to come to this group, and so I always invite those who appear to be unhappy to be there to leave if they'd like and return if and when they might want to. On occasion patients take advantage of this invitation to leave, and I've never seen it fail: They return when they have had a chance to get all their anger out, let go of their bravado, and allow the miracle of healing to enter their lives.

At the end of the day comes the meeting for recovering health care professionals, called the "caduceus" meeting after the winged staff with snakes that is the symbol of medicine. I'm particularly fond of this meeting because it attracts professionals in our local community who are in long-term recovery. It's always a pleasure to see them come in and share their experience, strength, and hope with our patients who have just arrived and are filled with fear.

At least 50 percent of this group is over fifty. As medical professionals, the attendees are well set in their ways, many of them with years of medical experience and well-fortified egos and senses of entitlement. But in this group among their peers, these men and women become equals, regardless of whether they are a medical student or a thirty-year veteran thoracic surgeon. Here the miracle of the Twelve Step recovery program takes place. The older adults are a treasured facet of this composition. As time goes on, they are often sought out after the meeting by younger people in the group to be mentors or sponsors. The spirituality and the grace, dignity, and appropriate benefits of eldership are applied to those individuals who have earned it, and it is a joy to see them bask in that light.

In this setting, I watch the fading away of the malignant shame that most of these older adults had and were weighed down with. At this point in their journey of recovery, they have accepted their addiction as a fatal disease, something they have to manage one day at a time. They have made their amends and taken the opportunity to heal relationships that were affected by their drug and alcohol abuse, by their anger and resentment and their power differential, thereby melting their shame and resentment away.

At the end of the day, I hit the computer, trying to finish up chart work that is required before I can go home. As rewarding as helping people find a new life in recovery can be, it consumes a lot of my energy. Arriving home to my beautiful wife, Nicolette, and our kittens, fish, frogs, and other creatures is always the highlight of my day. I always have a ritualistic cleansing, whether it's a swim in the pool, soaking in the hot tub, a yoga session, or just a hot shower. It's important for me to remove the stress and strain of the day while I enjoy the blessings of my own recovery at home with my family. That 4:00 a.m. wakeup call demands an early bedtime so it's a rare night when I'm up beyond 10 or 10:30. I try to center my mind, my soul and my spirit for an evening prayer and a good night's sleep to reenergize. Another group of new patients will be arriving in the morning.

■

CHAPTER 9

Helping Yourself

After fifty years of drinking casually, and then not so casually, Miriam's husband was in treatment. Up until a few years ago, the couple had had a wonderful life together. Social and outgoing, they liked to entertain as well as attend community events and parties. Cocktails and champagne seemed to follow them around. Miriam thoroughly enjoyed this lifestyle. So did her husband, until he found himself heading down to their personal wine cellar late every evening and drinking a bottle or two alone, on top of what he'd already had at dinner or a party with Miriam.

Miriam agreed to go to the family program, but she was angry and upset. He had embarrassed her in front of friends when he could no longer drink socially like her—a glass of wine or a cocktail or two. Normally easygoing and jovial, he had become easily agitated and distracted to the point of being rude. His behavior ruined her time at the social events, they stopped throwing their own parties, and then the two of them stopped socializing with others altogether. His disease had progressed to points that she had never thought possible—and it was robbing her of friends and community.

At the family program, Miriam learned that her husband was sick, that his alcoholism was a disease, and that he couldn't stop drinking on his own. She gained a new perspective as she came to understand the disease and listened to her husband plead with her that he had tried to control it and to maintain their lifestyle but couldn't. Miriam learned to forgive him. The family program also introduced Miriam to Al-Anon, a Twelve Step program for the friends and families of alcoholics, where she now goes on a regular basis while her husband attends his Alcoholics Anonymous meetings. Once again, they have a wonderful life. She can drink normally and does so with friends but no longer drinks in the house. Occasionally the couple even throws a party serving only nonalcoholic beverages. The couple found that they didn't lose their old community and that they gained a new community of friends through the Twelve Step programs.

■

Family members are usually the last to realize that their parent is addicted, the last to understand that the parent or grandparent needs help, the last to comprehend how much addiction has affected the entire family, and absolutely the last to seek help for themselves. Family members get caught up in the turmoil. Their focus is on the addict, who seems to demand a lot of negative attention. And, like the addict, family members are also prone to denial.

Whether we realize it or not, all families with addiction suffer. And most families, afraid of the stigma associated with the disease, are masters at hiding it from the outside world, which adds to the isolation and shame every family member is likely to experience.

Impact Based on Family Structure

The degree to which an older adult addict affects family, friends, or caregivers depends in part on how emotionally and physically close the addict is to everyone. The ninety-year-old lying in bed in a nursing home addicted to benzodiazepines is less likely to rule the roost than an unemployed sixty-year-old living in a multigenerational home. Yet an addicted grandmother who lives in Florida and is very close emotionally to her daughter's family in New Jersey can have a harrowing impact on her daughter's well-being—which trickles down to how she treats her husband and children—especially since distance allows for secrecy and limits how much the daughter can help.

The Multigenerational Home

When an addict of any age or relation lives in our house, a constant fog of fear, chaos, and anxiety is likely to eventually infiltrate every room and soul, creating an unbearable environment of unpredictability that sometimes feels like insanity. When the addict is an older adult and our parent, the impact takes on its own confusing twist. When things get bad enough, our role morphs from daughter or son to parent, disciplinarian, and rule setter. You withhold financial support after learning that Dad has squandered his retirement on illegal painkillers when his doctor refused to prescribe them anymore and has resorted to stealing from the kids' bank accounts. Mom's afternoon nip isn't funny anymore when you have to resort to taking the car keys before she can drive to the store, knowing full well she will stop for a long happy hour on the way back. Your parents, once pillars of integrity, are now lying about things as basic as what they're doing or where they're going. Being constantly subjected to an onslaught of lies leads to loss of trust, loss of control, and loss of respect. No longer knowing what to do, you throw up our hands. You might even feel like booting Mom or Dad out of the house.

Much like helping our parents with their showers and hygiene, this role reversal is at first confusing, even embarrassing. The awkwardness in giving our parents consequences for their behavior—and possibly doing it in front of our own children—makes us look and feel like control freaks. We loathe ourselves for losing our temper with our parent, yet we despise our parent's behavior even more. We've been taught to respect our elders, and if we want our children to uphold these same values, we're even more confused.

We find ourselves behaving anything but respectfully. We wonder how our kids, who witness our outbursts, will treat us later in life.

With addiction in the household, rifts between family members grow. A husband may blow off his father-in-law's excessive drinking as no big deal: "He's in his seventies. Let him enjoy his last years! He's not hurting anyone." On the other hand, the daughter bears the stress of watching her father, once her beacon of strength, stumble to bed every night, his health needlessly deteriorating before her and her children's eyes. Frustrated by her helplessness, she begins self-medicating with a glass or two of wine every night, arguing with her husband for not doing anything to make things better, and losing patience with the children. The kids, who used to enjoy fishing with Grandpa or seeing him in the stands at their football games, miss out on the irreplaceable love and support of their grandparent. Filled with shame, they are embarrassed to have him at their graduation party and secretly hope he'll forget and be at the bar that afternoon.

As the addiction progresses, family dynamics deteriorate. It used to be that the youngest in the family ruled the roost by naturally demanding the most attention. But now the center of attention becomes the person who is the unhealthiest—the aging addict—and at everyone else's expense. Instead of inviting neighbors over for an afternoon barbecue, family members would rather shut their doors and watch reruns, secure in the knowledge that Grandpa won't have an opportunity to embarrass everyone. Instead of helping Johnny prepare for college entrance exams, Mom is preoccupied with making sure her dad isn't going to get another DUI. The grandchildren absorb the stress and anxiety. Eventually, they give up hope of ever playing an important role in the family, or they rebel as a way to vie for attention.

You may not have these exact situations, but if you have an older adult addict living in your home, it's likely that what started out as a dream of being a loving and supportive multigenerational family can turn into a nightmare. Worry, anger, complete loss of control over the situation, fruitless shouting matches, slamming doors, and sleepless nights often consume families. The effect on those close to the addict is monumental and life changing: isolation, shame, anxiety, and loss. Lots of loss.

When You Are the Primary Caregiver of an Ailing Addict

Whether you live in a full house or alone with Mom or another older adult, if you are taking care of an older adult with health or mental health issues and addiction, you may feel that your job is around the clock, as you attend to health, hygiene, and the consequences of addiction (or potential addiction) simultaneously. Burnout is inevitable—and in short order. It can be hard enough caring for an older adult when addiction isn't in the picture.

The pain medication Dad has been on for five years has long stopped working, and Dad's pain is unbearable, even though his doctor keeps upping the dosage. Mom recently started taking Valium and Lunesta, and you notice her dementia is worsening. You come home from work in the evening to find that she's left the stove burner on since breakfast. On another occasion, the front door is wide open, but no one is home.

You fear that Dad is always going to suffer or that you can't leave Mom home alone anymore. Doctors keep prescribing medication, no one is getting better, and you feel worse and worse: helpless, stressed, and confused about what to do. The words *misuse* or *addiction* may have never entered your mind. And why should they? Mom and Dad are aging, and their bodies and minds are beginning to fail them. While this may be true, it's also true that Dad is addicted to pain medication and can be helped, and Mom's drug combination is exacerbating or even causing her dementia. You, the primary caregiver, are struggling in every sense—emotionally, mentally, physically, and perhaps financially. Mom and Dad can most likely be helped. Mom's medication can be adjusted, and Dad can enter a reputable pain management program and experience some amazing results. As for you, some well-deserved self-care is in order.

When Dad Lives Far Away

Perhaps nothing is more anxiety provoking than long-distance caregiving. You know only a fraction of the story, hear bits and pieces from neighbors and friends, receive the occasional alarming call from a sibling, and are astonished at your loved one's decline since the last time you saw him in person a year ago. If Mom is taking care of Dad, she may say that Dad is doing fine, all in an effort to protect you. Or she may call once a week in hysterics, alarming you without real cause in an effort to guilt you into being around more often. Perhaps you are still raising a family of your own, have established strong roots in your community, or have a job you cannot up and leave at a moment's notice. You spend most of your vacation and sick time visiting your folks. Still, the guilt of not being there for your parents is in the backdrop of every conversation you have (or don't have).

The Parent Who Didn't Take Care of You

If addiction is familiar to you because you grew up with it, and your addicted parent now needs your help with caregiving or treatment and recovery, you may have strong reservations about getting involved. You may flat out refuse. You've been there and done that. Dad wasn't there for you, and you sure as hell aren't going to be there for him.

Helping a parent who never bothered to help you can be the greatest act of forgiveness you ever do. It can also be nearly impossible for you to fathom and even more impossible to carry out. Do not put yourself or your parent in a position you can't handle.

Everyone in this situation faces a unique set of demons. Your pain may run deeper than you realize. If you're struggling with taking care of a parent who didn't take care of you, you can lighten your load considerably by seeking support—ideally from a professional who understands addiction as well as all the issues of caregiving for an older adult. These are two of the hardest—and most worthy—issues you will ever address. I highly recommend professional support, which can expedite your healing process by Mach speed.

Elder Abuse

I include this section on elder abuse to heighten awareness. In 1996, the National Elder Abuse Incidence Study revealed that about a half million older adults in the United States suffered from abuse in domestic settings (this does not include nursing homes or other care facilities). Abuse can be physical, sexual, verbal, or some form of exploitation, including financial and even medication misuse. But these were only the reported incidents. The study estimated that for every reported incident, another five cases went unreported. As the number of older adults (age sixty-five and older) increases—from about 43 million as of this writing to nearly 84 million projected in 2050 (including the last of the boomers, expected to reach age eighty-five)—so does the potential for elder abuse. The study also found that those over age eighty are two to three times more likely to be abused. In 90 percent of the cases where the perpetrator is known, the perpetrator is a family member, usually an adult child or a spouse.[39]

Few things are more heartbreaking than abuse. Abuse is power over someone who's vulnerable, whether a child, adult, or older adult. Be aware. If your loved one has suspicious bruises or broken bones, is missing money or prescription pills, or if you have other reason to suspect abuse, call the adult protective services agency in the appropriate state. If you think your loved one is in immediate danger, dial 911.

The Three Cs

Regardless of your caregiving situation, the solution is the same. You and your family need help, whether you realize it or not. One of the first steps for you is to understand the "three Cs" concept: You didn't *cause* the addiction, you can't *control* the addiction, and you can't *cure* it. No matter what you do to try to force your loved one to stop drinking or taking pills, you will most likely end up frustrated and angry.

Addiction takes on a life of its own. The addict loses control over his or her use, becomes obsessed with using, and develops a tolerance for the drug of choice. The only surefire way to help the addict is to get help for yourself first and foremost, so that you can learn the tools and strategies necessary to escape the isolation and shame and enter into a healthier relationship, full of boundaries and self-regard, with the addict. Then, and only then, can you realize the impact addiction has had on you and your family and how helpless you truly are over the disease.

Recovery for the Family

You've been running around like a chicken with your head cut off trying to manage the consequences of your loved one's addiction. If and when he or she finally goes through treatment, your job isn't over, as you might need to help your loved one manage their recovery, as well as your own. Yes, you and each of your family members need to recover, too. To be successful, you will need to learn some new tools and strategies. These methods were first introduced to family members of addicts in 1936, when Lois Wilson, wife of Bill Wilson, co-founder of Alcoholics Anonymous (AA), had informal meetings with the wives of the alcoholics in her home. In the earliest days of AA, it was already clear that family members needed just as much help and support as alcoholics. Their behavior had changed in response to addiction. They had tried to control what they could not, felt shame because of the stigma, and were isolated in an effort to conceal their pain.

What does recovery for the family involve? Following is a short list of steps family members can take to begin to heal:

- Accept that you and your family, not only the addict, need to recover from the insanity that is addiction.
- Connect with others who are in the same boat as you.
- Learn new ways of communicating with the addict and other family members.
- Detach with love.
- Take responsibility for your actions.
- Be grateful for what is good in your life.
- Engage the entire family in recovery efforts.
- Begin new family activities that do not involve drugs or alcohol.
- Expect lifelong recovery, but prepare for relapse.

Outlets for Help

Recovering alone from the family disease of addiction can be likened to isolating during active addiction. It isn't very effective, and it isn't any fun. Although your circumstances are unique, millions of others have gone or are going through the same type of ordeal. They share the same feelings and frustrations. Their support can be everything to you and your recovery.

Support groups such as Al-Anon, Nar-Anon, and Alateen are widespread. You'll likely find a meeting in your neighborhood or close by (see al-anon.org or nar-anon.org for information). Caregiving support groups are growing in number as well. You can usually find one at your local hospital or community center, or visit AARP's Caregiving Resource Center at aarp.org/caregiving. Although it can be hard for some of us to admit we need help, to talk in a group setting, or to take the time to get to a meeting, there's no better time to take a leap of faith. Select a meeting and give it a try. Attend at least five meetings before giving up on it. If at that point it still doesn't resonate with you, pick another meeting. Eventually, you'll probably connect, and once you do, you'll find yourself looking forward to the next meeting.

Getting professional help is also an option. If your parent is not in treatment or recovery, and if you do not already see a therapist or counselor, check online for clinicians in your area who specialize in addiction. Some addiction treatment clinics or centers offer outpatient mental health services. Call and inquire about whom you could see for family recovery. Getting help from a professional doesn't have to be a lifelong obligation. Some people find amazing relief and clarity after one or two appointments.

Family programs are specifically tailored to family members of addicts and alcoholics. Some treatment centers open their program to the public, regardless of whether they have or had a loved one in treatment at the center. The bonds created among families at these programs are sometimes lifelong.

If you have a religious affiliation, talk with your clergy, priest, rabbi, or other spiritual leader. They are likely to have heard the story before. If they know your family, they may already know more than you realize. If they don't know your family well, they will welcome the opportunity to get to know you. Most religious leaders have become sophisticated about addiction and recognize it as a no-fault disease, although some may still see addiction as a failure of will or a sin, and will only feed the shame that you or your loved one is feeling. In that case, you might shop around for a church or temple where you can find the enlightened support you need.

Whether religious, Twelve Step, or otherwise, retreats are an excellent venue for finding peace and tranquility. Talk to your place of worship or treatment center, or look online. If you can't get away but feel you need to, brainstorm with family, friends, clergy, or others on how to arrange a weekend away.

Self-care is not selfish. If you don't already meditate, exercise, do yoga, journal, take walks in nature, or engage in other health-promoting activities, pick one or more and start slowly. Schedule it into your day. Even focusing on deep breathing for one minute a day is a start to a meditation ritual. Making a habit of smiling once a day can change your outlook. Writing a short gratitude list every night can do wonders.

These suggestions are the tip of the iceberg. Hundreds of books, tapes, and even apps are available to help you navigate the rough waters of addiction and stay on track in recovery. Check online or in the recovery section of your local bookstore. The resource section in the back of this book can get you started. And remember, you are not alone.

■

CHAPTER 10

Staying on Track in Recovery

Jim, now seventy-five years old, tells people he was nearly "a goner" when his family put him in treatment at age seventy-two, and he isn't joking. Shortly after he was admitted into the treatment facility, he was transferred to a hospital for intensive treatment of liver failure. To complicate matters, Jim was so confused and belligerent that his family thought he had permanently "lost his mind." After a month in the hospital, his physical condition had improved enough for him to be transferred to a rehab facility. He spent sixty days there before getting well enough to enter treatment for alcoholism. During his treatment stint, Jim says he came back to life. "You can call me Lazarus," says Jim, referring to the Biblical story where Jesus brings a dead man back to life.

Jim now has a profound sense of gratitude for his miraculous second chance at life. Like so many older adults who discover sobriety, he has a renewed sense of energy and purpose. Jim and his older peers in recovery do not doubt that sobriety is a second chance at life. These are the people who embrace all of life that they can: They renew marriage vows, repair damaged family relationships, get remarried, return part time to previous careers, and find interesting volunteer opportunities. Older people in recovery are markedly determined to make each day count.

Family members were amazed to see Jim's surge in accomplishments, spiritual growth, and self-identity. From Jim's old life, he still retains a cane and small limp, but his new outlook on life is contagious. He motivates peers and younger people alike. Jim says, "My life is beyond my wildest imagination. I am doing things I had only hoped to do as a kid."

■

Many older adults in early recovery are like Jim. They're fully alive and ready to take the bull by the horns. They've been around long enough to know that a second chance like this doesn't come around every day. They take full advantage of it and never look back.

But everyone isn't like Jim. Staying on track in recovery is harder. Some people don't like change, they crave their drug of choice, and they complain of pain.

Let's say that you, on the other hand, are ready to sigh in relief. Your loved one is out of treatment, off mood-altering drugs, taking only the prescribed medications that are absolutely necessary, and has started being his normal self again. Even if he isn't jumping with joy, his health, mood, memory, and outlook are far better than they were before treatment. But you can't quite allow yourself to fully relax. There's good reason for this hesitancy. First, you've gone through a lot. It's hard to trust that the worry, headache, and stress are over—that life with your loved one is truly going to get better. Second, whether you fully realize it or not, in some ways, the hard part has just begun.

Recognizing, admitting to, and getting treated for addiction are some of the hardest steps anyone will ever take in life. They are the monumental moments, when energy and support are most profound, fueled by anxiety, relief, fear, and joy—all at the same time. During the first few months of recovery, daily life starts all over again. Energy levels return to normal, which, for some, spells complacency.

You may be expecting the best. You've got the knowledge and tools you need to help your loved one stay in recovery. Yet it's also important to consider that emotions may be on edge, old daily regimens and ruts can resurface, and "triggers" to drink or use can abound.

Early recovery is not the time to let your guard down. It's a time to expect the best and prepare for the worst. The addict in early recovery is adjusting. But so are you, as well as friends, caregivers, employers, and everyone else. Loved ones and caregivers might find themselves walking on eggshells or waiting for the other shoe to drop. It takes a nanosecond to lose someone's trust, but it can take a lifetime to rebuild it. At this point, the older adult is just laying the foundation.

Recovery, in other words, is a process. It is, at first, a moment-to-moment process and then eventually a day-by-day process. Treatment ends but recovery does not—remember this is a chronic disease that requires lifelong maintenance. Every day is an opportunity to work on being more fulfilled in recovery. Those in Twelve Step programs find fulfillment through the principles of honesty, faith, surrender, courage, humility, justice, vigilance, awareness, integrity, and finally service and charity. Yet every day also offers an opportunity to slip—which in recovery terms means to take a drink, a toke, or an unnecessary pill—or to fall into a full-blown relapse.

In this chapter, we're going to take a look at some of the issues that can arise in early recovery, and I'm going to point out where you need to be stringent when it comes to older adults in particular. The issues will vary, depending on the age of the older adult. The fifty-five-year-old husband in recovery is in a different place than the eighty-year-old mom in recovery. They have the same disease, but they most likely have entirely different situations. I'll cover what you can expect from your loved one in recovery, some tried-and-true methods for dealing with some of the more difficult times, and what you can do to help prevent relapse.

The good news—and there is a lot of good news in recovery—is that compared to their younger counterparts, older adults have a better chance of staying in recovery.

Real-Life Reactions

When Dad is in recovery, abstaining from mood-altering drugs, not everyone is necessarily going to be as overjoyed as you are. His buddies at the rec center are going to miss him at four o'clock happy hour. Mom might even be a little bothered when Dad, missing his afternoon ritual, starts fidgeting at about 3:30. Mom might even get upset when Dad spends almost every evening attending Alcoholics Anonymous meetings instead of enjoying a leisurely meal with her. And where are all these new AA friends coming from? Why does he spend so much time on the phone with them? He seems to enjoy the company of his sponsor more than her.

And then there's the big one—mistrust. Even if Dad is truly attending AA meetings and going out for coffee afterward, Mom has good reason from past behavior to believe he's not telling the truth. She has, after all, been lied to before. When she confronts him, he's dumbfounded. He is, after all, doing what she's wanted him to do for years. The stress of all these changes can at times be almost as challenging as life was when Dad was drinking.

Recovery changes things, and change requires adjustment, even if we normally thrive on it. In cases like this, Mom benefits from attending a support group, too. Al-Anon and Nar-Anon are made for family members of alcoholics and drug addicts (whether in recovery or not). Attending support groups can turn a bomb waiting to explode into a dud. It can also set off some fireworks of enlightenment. To boot, Mom develops her own new network of friends. Life expands, and Mom and Dad eventually begin to embrace their new world.

Triggers and Cravings

Seventy-year-old William has always been social and extroverted. His neighbors love to chat with him, and local business owners are happy when he stops in for coffee, groceries, or handyman supplies. William is well known in local bars and restaurants also, but he is known to hold his liquor well and never cause trouble. William's wife and grown children know otherwise. William recently completed treatment, and he is feeling good about the experience—mostly good, that is.

When William and his wife go to their favorite Mexican restaurant, they are welcomed by familiar wait staff and regular customers. No menus are needed, because William and his wife always order the same food and drinks. As soon as William walks in the door, warm food smells envelop him. His friends are drinking beer, and the salted edges of margarita glasses look positively wonderful. The absence of alcohol at home has not bothered William, but suddenly William feels stressed and nervous. He and his wife sit down, order sodas and food, but William doesn't enjoy the meal. A pitcher of beer would really taste great, he keeps thinking.

■

Jocelyn is sixty-four and not quite retired. Her employer recently sent her to treatment for dependence on prescription pain medicine, and she feels confident that she has the support and tools to stay in recovery. Jocelyn works for a large school district and feels positive and energetic while at work. The weekends, however, seem long and lonely. She goes home to a quiet house, and her grown children are busy with their own lives. Her husband died two years earlier.

Weekend nights are endless for Jocelyn. She could go to a movie or school sporting event, but she doesn't want to go alone. She starts to feel sad and anxious, and remembers why her medications offered such solace on a Saturday night. She calls her daughter, but no one answers. She calls a friend who answers but has company to entertain. She opens the cabinet where she stores tea and coffee, and reaches for the tea kettle. Her eyes wander to the cabinet where her medications used to sit. She opens the cabinet and finds only clean cups and glasses. She imagines opening a pill bottle and dropping pills onto her palm.

■

Because addiction, including alcoholism, is a chronic disease, even if a person has successfully made it through early recovery, many things can trigger cravings. Those triggers might be certain people who always drank or smoked weed with the person. Certain places, like bars or sporting events, might trigger the urge to use. Certain routines might trigger the desire to drink or return to prescription drug use. Certain times of day or rituals might trigger someone to crave the relief promised by an old prescription.

In treatment, people are taught to identify people, places, and things that might be triggers to use. Once out of treatment those triggers can be insidious. Maybe William didn't know that going to a Mexican restaurant—something he associated with family and friends—would cause him to feel crabby and cheated of enjoyment. Now that he knows, William needs to take note of the experience and use the tools he learned about in treatment. Perhaps he and his wife could find a new restaurant, but he would definitely be wise to discuss his craving for beer with his sponsor and therapist. Secrets keep us sick. Transparency is ever so important in recovery.

Jocelyn is finding out that quiet weekends are a trigger for her. Her support system is not as strong as it could be, so she also needs to use tools she learned about in treatment. Isolating and looking in the cabinet where she once stored her pills are dangerous triggers for Jocelyn. She needs to talk to her sponsor about planning her weekends, and keep her sponsor and her therapist informed of cravings and triggers that haunt her.

Slips and Relapses

What happens if our loved one has a beer, joint, or pill in recovery? Have all the time, effort, money, and energy that went into getting her clean and sober been a waste of time? In some cases, slips have the effect of strengthening recovery because the addict may finally be convinced that she really can't control her use. The National Institute on Drug Abuse (NIDA) frames a relapse this way:

> Similar to other chronic, relapsing diseases, such as diabetes, asthma, or heart disease, drug addiction can be managed successfully. And as with other chronic diseases, it is not uncommon for a person to relapse and begin abusing drugs again. Relapse, however, does not signal treatment failure—rather, it indicates that treatment should be reinstated or adjusted or that an alternative treatment is needed to help the individual regain control and recover.[40]

Having a drink or a pill in recovery is called a slip. A slip is usually unplanned. The brain—still healing from drug toxicity—acts on impulse. With a slip, we might have one night on the town and wake up to realize what a horrible mistake we've made. We call our sponsor, attend AA meetings every day for two weeks, and perhaps write about our thinking that led to the slip in a journal. We do what we need to do to get back on track. We fortify our recovery plan—attend more meetings, widen our support group, take up new activities. A return to using shows us where the hole is in our program. A slip can make us and our program stronger.

Relapse, compared to a slip, can also make us stronger, but it brings us down farther. A relapse is more serious, but it doesn't start with a drink. Relapse begins long before we take the first drink and is first reflected in our behavior and attitude. We start feeling bored with recovery. We start having lunch at the bar we used to frequent, feeling we can handle it. Rather than make efforts to bond with others in recovery, we start criticizing the people at our AA home group and complain that we don't fit in. We don't take responsibility for our behavior. Rather than apologize for speaking harshly to our wife, we blow it off, complaining that she's a nag and doesn't trust us.

All of these behaviors are taking us back to our old self, the one that drank or used. At this stage, once we do pick up a drink, we are not likely to stop after a night on the town. We tell ourselves we "deserve" to drink. This recovery stuff is stupid and too much effort. A full-blown relapse could have us drinking or using for a week, a month, a year, or the rest of our life.

Knowing that relapse starts with addictive thinking and behavior is beyond important. It's your first clue that something needs to change. A big part of treatment and recovery is relapse prevention.

Understanding the difference between a slip and relapse can help older adults allay feelings of shame and can assure you that, for some people, either or both are a natural part of the process of recovery from addiction. The same is true of other chronic diseases, like diabetes or hypertension. In other words, long-term recovery requires long-term efforts. Not everyone in recovery experiences slips or relapses, but a majority of recovering people do relapse.

Relapse does not happen because an older adult is weak or undisciplined. Relapse is part and parcel of a chronic disease. According to NIDA:

Addiction is a complex but treatable disease that affects brain function and behavior. Drugs of abuse alter the brain's structure and function, resulting in changes that persist long after drug use has ceased. This may explain why drug abusers are at risk for relapse even after long periods of abstinence and despite the potentially devastating consequences.[41]

PORTRAIT OF A RELAPSE

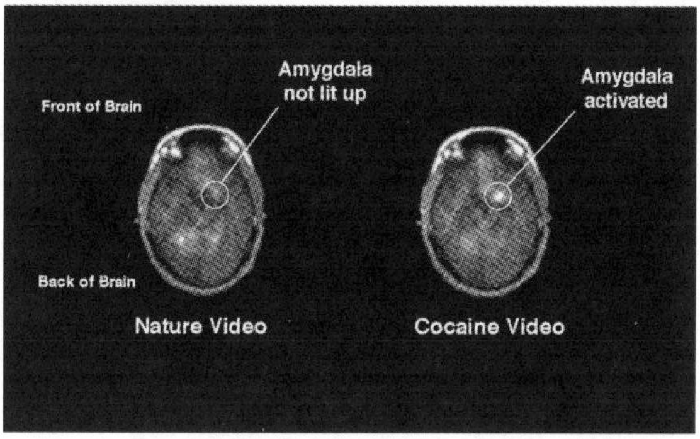

One of the most telling portraits of a relapse is found in the neuroimagery of a PET scan. These images show areas of normal glucose metabolism and the craving area of the brain of a cocaine addict who is in recovery. The addict has just been shown a video of nature photos, beautiful images that probably recount multiple memories of hiking or climbing or fishing. Oddly, the reward center of the addict's brain is quiet; there is no stimulation. Next, the same addict is shown a picture of someone with a straw up his nose, snorting any substance. It could be sugar, it could be talcum powder—it could be anything. And just the mere imagery of the inhalation of the drug or a tourniquet on the arm or the smoking of a drug stimulates the brain's reward center. The colors change vibrantly in this area called the amygdala. It is on fire. The image is a visual representation of the neurochemical, biological nature of a relapse.

It's important to know that relapses are not about character or even bad judgment, but they are about people, places, and things that stimulate the memory banks and activate the stress mechanisms in the reward area of this wonderful computer we call the brain. The brain, now lit up, actively seeks a substance that will add the chemicals the brain so deeply requires—in this case, dopamine. The mere smell of whiskey, hearing a favorite old song, the tinkle of ice cubes in glasses, sounds of bottles opening, or the feel of an icy cold beer mug, whether it contains root beer or nonalcoholic beer or cream soda, may stimulate that part of the brain. Although an alcoholic may drink the root beer or cream soda with some satisfaction, that area of the brain is not satisfied. It's looking for something more, and it is bent on finding it.

These very dangerous situations are the people, places, and things we talk about that can be triggers for a relapse, and the older adult has many memories and experiences that can also act as triggers—the familiarity of a family reunion, a traditional holiday celebration, and old drinking buddies at the veteran's hall. Relapse is a biochemical event.

Sometimes it's helpful if people relocate after treatment to avoid powerful triggers, but not everyone has that option. Even if they do, moving away isn't a cure-all. Some people in recovery will tell you that once they stopped using, they never looked back. For others, triggers are everywhere and cravings are powerful. They can even pop up ten years into a solid recovery. Be aware that triggers exist and that your loved one or patient may need your compassion and your help when they arise.

I think that loved ones can look at the lives of an older adult and find those rewarding and wonderful things that are meaningful and not remotely associated with a choice. Playing with his grandchildren, talking with her pastor at church on Sunday, gardening, watching a movie, holding hands with a spouse or child, looking through family albums. These may sound somewhat bor-ing at first, but for the older adult they decrease stress levels and act almost as antitriggers. Simply giving of your time, a smile, or uncomplicated listening to a story you heard twenty times before may give the older adult that clarity, that peace, where their demons are put to rest and cravings, as well as the power behind the triggers, subside.

COMMON SIGNS AND SYMPTOMS OF RELAPSE

Relapse comes in the form of thoughts and behaviors that begin long before we take a drink or use a drug. Some common signs are as follows:

- Argumentativeness
- Avoidance
- Believing it can't happen to me
- Blaming
- Cockiness
- Complacency
- Confusion
- Crisis building
- Defensiveness
- Denial
- Depression
- Dishonesty
- Excuse making
- Exhaustion
- Expecting too much from the program
- Feeling omnipotent
- Feeling stuck in the program
- Feeling trapped, suicidal, or insane
- Forgetting to be grateful
- High expectations
- Impatience
- Irresponsibility
- Isolation
- Lack of discipline
- Loss of control
- Neglecting personal hygiene
- Obsessing about using the substance
- Panic/anxiety
- Poor me
- Restlessness, irritability, discontentment
- Risk taking
- Self-pity
- Switching "poisons (excessive" behaviors around gambling, food, sex, or work)
- Use of a mood-altering substance

Meetings and Mentorship

Recovery requires a new way of living. Not everyone gets excited about shaking things up in their world, and some older adults seem to be particularly reluctant since routine is often important to them. Most older adults I've worked with benefit from finding a new routine, especially if they can play the very useful role of mentor to younger addicts and alcoholics. This is where the joy lies for many addicts.

AA, NA, and other Twelve Step programs and non–Twelve Step peer support groups, such as SMART Recovery and Women for Sobriety, offer a place where addicts can both give and get support for living a sober lifestyle in a safe, structured setting that encourages privacy and anonymity. Groups built around the Twelve Steps have helped millions of people remain abstinent from mood-altering drugs since the late 1930s. There are AA meetings everywhere in the world, made up of people from every walk of life. There are special population meetings, for example, for women, older adults, Hispanics, and gays and lesbians, which are more likely to be available in larger communities. There are different kinds of meetings as well, including speaker meetings where members share their stories of experience, strength, and hope; Big Book meetings where the AA textbook, *Alcoholics Anonymous*, is studied; and Step or topic meetings, where members volunteer to lead the group in talking about a different Step or related topic each meeting. There is generally an unspoken rule of no "cross-talk" (giving feedback), which can be especially comforting to older adult newcomers who aren't looking for advice from just anybody and simply want to have a place to share their thoughts and feelings about staying sober.

As mentioned earlier, it is important for newcomers to find a sponsor, someone in the program who has had at least two years of sobriety and is the same gender (except for gay or lesbian members, who are advised to find someone of the opposite gender). Like AA's co-founders, Bill W. and Dr. Bob, the original sponsor and sponsee who stayed sober because they were one alcoholic talking to another, sponsors play a mentorship role and are rewarded in return by being able to carry the message of recovery. I think it's useful for older adults to have a sponsor close to their own age with whom they can share some of the special challenges that older people in recovery face. After being in the program for a while, working the Steps, and getting some stable sobriety, older adults can bring their mountains of experience to being a sponsor themselves. They may find that they have a lot they can share with younger people in the group who will value an older person's perspective gained through years of life experience.

The first meetings may be difficult, especially until the older adult finds the right group with the right chemistry. A group with other older people can make getting comfortable easier, as can finding a gender-specific group, especially for women. The best way to adapt is with repetition, allowing the comfort of ritual and familiarity with the people to grow with time. Addicts should go to multiple meetings per week at first, if that is practical, and once established, at least one meeting weekly. When they have found a group that they like, they can make it their "home group" and build supportive relationships over time, which can include socializing before and after meetings.

Challenge the Practitioner

Everyone needs an advocate now and then. Chances are good that the older adult you care for is already working with a health care provider. Whether the person is seeing one primary care physician for biannual checkups or visiting multiple physicians monthly, you will want to ensure that each physician who treats your loved one is aware that he or she is in recovery and that any mood-altering substance could cause relapse. In chapter 11, I'll cover the special monitoring necessary for adults who need mood-altering pain medication. I cannot emphasize enough the importance of staying on top of what's being prescribed, how often, what it's for, and why. Most doctors are not adequately trained in addiction medicine. During all their years of training, they often receive only four hours of training on addiction. You'd have to live under a rock not to know that painkillers have become one of the most deadly legal substances ever prescribed on such a wide scale. Doctors don't live under rocks, but they do follow medical protocols when it comes to treating patient pain. If a protocol involves prescribing painkillers, you must advocate, advocate, advocate. If you're not satisfied with the results, visit the American Society for Addiction Medicine website and, if possible, find a doctor certified in addiction medicine whom you can go to. These doctors are fully trained in addiction science and are growing in numbers. Otherwise, if advocacy and education don't work with your doctor, shop around until you find a doctor who will listen.

Physicians make life-and-death decisions almost daily. They are usually knowledgeable, powerful, and busy, and not always willing or able to take the time to explain their decisions to family members. You may feel that it's not your place to question a doctor's orders. They're the experts, after all. It's not only okay, it is absolutely necessary that you challenge the practitioner if and when you believe your loved one is vulnerable to relapse because of addictive medication or an unhealthy mix of prescriptions.

Hand-in-hand with advocacy are ongoing drug audits, which we discussed earlier. For your loved one, this process does not end when she is sober. Ongoing drug audits will help your loved-one stay on track and give you peace of mind.

Having a Plan

Successful recovery requires planning. A relapse prevention plan is a set of actions you, the older adult, family members, bosses, caregivers—anyone involved in the person's recovery—can automatically put into motion if relapse is imminent, or even if you suspect something is just a little off. Signs of relapse include everything from not wanting to go to Twelve Step meetings to having a urine test that's positive for opioids. A relapse prevention plan is a written agreement that holds older adults and those who care for them accountable for their actions and behaviors.

The beauty of a relapse prevention plan is that everything is spelled out—everyone knows the best course of action to take in any given situation. You don't have to panic. You don't have to pull your hair out or break down. You simply pick up the plan and do what you know you need to do.

If the older adult you care for has not gone through treatment, you can find various templates for plans online and make your own. Your loved one's sponsor might also have some good suggestions. A good plan is agreed to by the addict and others in advance—it's a signed contract in writing.

Our Resilient Brains and Bodies

One of the great gifts given to human beings is a remarkably resilient brain and resilient body. If we don't go over that final line, where irreversibility of disease process takes place, the amount of recovery possible for any human being continues to amaze me. I have never seen an area of medicine where more miracles are possible than in the field of addiction and recovery. Whether it be a twenty-four-year-old girl on her way to having cirrhosis of the liver or an older adult with cognitive impairment from years of drinking and drugging, our ability to heal over time with the support of others and a commitment to a rigorous program of recovery is truly awe inspiring.

The question becomes what will we do with this miraculous gift of healing? Almost any addict in recovery will tell you sobriety is not to be taken for granted but to be cherished one day at a time. One of the best ways to show our gratitude is to take care of ourselves—physically, mentally, emotionally, and spiritually.

Older adults today have a lot of options when it comes to exercise programs, stress reduction, and easy access to healthy food choices. Many fitness centers now welcome older adults by offering Silver Sneakers programs, special weight training regimens, yoga, water aerobics, and more. Help to ensure that the older adult stays as active as possible. Movement and stretching prevent illness, increase balance, and improve healing in every aspect. I cannot emphasize this enough.

Older addicts also benefit from the scientific research now being done that shows how changing our thinking can influence health, behavior, and more. And as the baby boomer generation continues to age, and older adults become a significantly visible age group, we can expect more options, more research, and less ageism. This generation is simply too large to ignore.

Earlier in this book I talked about chronological versus biological age. Some ninety-year-olds have healthier hearts than fifty-year-olds. Age is not just a number but a mind-set. How we think of ourselves and aging in general affects how we age. For example, if we keep saying no one will hire us because we're too old, that's probably what will happen. If we act and behave as if we add value because of our age, we might find job offers pouring in. Aging is a frame of mind. What you believe affects how you behave and how others perceive you.

Lastly, what good is recovery if it is not being enjoyed? Studies show that centenarians live long not because they take a lot of pills. They stay active, celebrate successes, surround themselves with supportive people, and savor life's little joys—a hot cup of tea, a baby's smile, a bar of chocolate. If all this is true, then the support and wisdom available in the Twelve Step program of recovery is a recipe for living to a ripe old age.

We now need to look at healthy ways to be pain-free and drug-free in recovery.

■

CHAPTER 11

Killing Pain Safely

Mary, age eighty-three, was looking forward to attending a friend's beautiful outdoor wedding ceremony. She had picked out the perfect outfit and was prepared to wear heels instead of her normal flat shoes. She had some mobility issues but knew if she took her medication as directed, the heels wouldn't affect her balance and she could maneuver the gravel driveway, uneven stone walkway, and lumpy grass terrain to the tent where the wedding and reception would be held. She did not adjust any of her medications, anticipating she might have some pain and discomfort in the outdoor setting. Two hours before the event, she took her pain medication.

The wedding ceremony was marvelous, and Mary was so happy to be in attendance. While waiting to sit down for dinner, she held engaging conversations with friends. As the waiter roamed the tent with a bottle of wine, she managed to drink two glasses without really being aware of it. Then there was the champagne wedding toast followed by several cocktails during the dinner. At the dance following dinner, she had a couple more cocktails. Meanwhile, she was very happy laughing with others and even danced to a few songs. While she was in this merry state, she was also on very dangerous turf.

Negotiating the grass and the driveway in her heels, she began to feel a little woozy. After all, on top of her pain medication, she had managed to consume four to five times her normal alcohol intake in that one day. As she was attempting to find her way to the ladies restroom, she stumbled and fell, hitting her head on the pavement. She was found unresponsive and bleeding by friends who called 911. The paramedics arrived and took her to the emergency room.

While she was able to go home after extensive testing and did not suffer any broken bones, the repercussions of that evening are with her still. She feels guilt and shame about drinking too much and being found on the pavement. She now isolates from others because she doesn't want to be known as the drunk at the wedding, although she typically doesn't drink much alcohol at all. To herself, she is a social outcast. She is devastated.

Mary's story is not atypical at all; I have seen it in my own practice a thousand times.

■

"But I Can't Take Mom's Pain Pills Away. I Don't Want Her to Suffer!"

Approximately one in four Americans—76.2 million people—have experienced chronic pain that lasts longer than twenty-four hours.[42] The numbers for acute, short-lasting pain are certainly much higher, given that almost everyone experiences it at one time or another. More people suffer from pain than from diabetes, heart disease, and cancer combined, and it's the main reason people visit the doctor, physical therapist, chiropractor, or other medical professional. Pain can stem from physical, emotional, or psychosocial circumstances. It can be acute or chronic. It can come and go. It can be sharp, dull, throbbing, piercing, intense, moderate, or mild. Pain is nearly universal, yet how we experience it is always personal. How do we treat something as common, complicated, and necessary, yet as unwanted as pain? Most important, how do we treat it safely?

Abstinence from all mood-altering drugs is a cornerstone of addiction treatment. What do you do if your loved one is about to enter treatment but is using prescribed narcotics to alleviate a painful condition? Narcotics, as we know, are highly mood altering, capable of creating a dreamy euphoria, at least in the beginning. We also learned that once the user's body begins to "tolerate" the drug, the dreamy effect is no longer within reach; it can only be chased—by increasing the dosage—but never caught. The drug user at this point might be addicted or on his way to becoming addicted. He was taking the drug at first to feel high and ends up taking it to "medicate" the withdrawal symptoms and feel normal as his brain loses its ability to manufacture the feel-good chemical, dopamine, naturally. How do you reconcile robbing your loved one, who may be in the twilight of life, of the chance to feel "normal"? Worse, how do you subject him to pain?

If your loved one is not going to treatment, you may be concerned that his prescription painkillers have outlived their purpose. You may be worried that addiction is just around the corner. Or maybe you live by the idiom that prevention is better than a cure and don't want to risk addiction to begin with. If it's weighing on your mind, it's most likely time to consider a supervised detoxification from narcotic painkillers, whether prescribed or not, and replacing them with nonnarcotic painkilling options. Here's why.

In chapter 4, I talked about this remarkable paradox: Painkillers can eventually cause pain. Once you begin to tolerate the drug, you've reached a tipping point of sorts. The medication stops serving you and begins to work against you. Anyone who takes opioid painkillers for an extended period (two to four weeks), whether for acute or chronic conditions, runs the risk of being trapped in an endless cycle: pain, use, withdrawal; pain, use, withdrawal. The cycle may have little to do with the physical ailment (backache or nerve pain, for instance) and everything to do with brain chemistry. Mood-altering painkillers, if you recall, hijack the brain's reward system.

The truth of the matter is, if you take a hundred patients who are on chronic pain medications and put them in a room, take away their chronic pain medications, and move them through three physical therapy pool exercises per day, a high percentage are going to feel better just because the opiates and the pain they produce (opioid-induced hyperalgesia) are gone. Other positive changes will happen as well: Normal bowel function will return as constipation vanishes; light headedness, an adverse consequence of over-sedation with other medications, disappears. Patients will be more alert, reflexes will improve, conversation will improve, thinking will improve, mental status overall will improve. I witness these results almost daily in the pain clinic at the Betty Ford Center. People at first are so remarkably surprised by the fact that the pain is lessened when they stop these medications that joy and hope continues to radiate from them and carries them through any pain that they might experience. They are getting better, and they know it. Many who come in wheelchairs, on stretchers, or using walkers leave our facility standing upright after three to five weeks of participating in yoga, stretching, and gym and pool exercises. It is quite remarkable what mindfulness, Qigong, and the alternative pain treatments that I refer to at the end of this chapter can do for someone who has walked into the prison of pain treatment.

No one wants to see their patients, parents, or loved ones suffer. Most of us cringe at the thought of being in pain. Some of us even feel it vicariously. But taking Mom's pills away doesn't have to mean suffering. On the contrary, with professional help, it often marks the beginning of healing.

What Is Pain?

Almost every living creature that has a nervous system (i.e., a brain) is capable of feeling pain, so unless you're an amoeba or a sea sponge, you will experience brain messages in reaction to painful stimuli. That is, if you place the palm of your hand on a hot stove, your brain will send pain signals to the palm of your hand. Your hand will hurt, and you will be inclined to quickly remove it from the hot stovetop before suffering a second- or third-degree burn. Your brain is, technically, causing the pain to prevent you from further damaging your hand—a limb the brain considers important enough to salvage.

Congenital insensitivity to pain (CIP) is a rare condition in which people are either insensitive (do not feel) or indifferent (are able to perceive stimulus but unable to react) to pain. In either case, the person does not pull her hand from the hot stovetop. The cause of CIP is thought to be a genetic mutation that results in an excess production of endorphins—those feel-good neurotransmitters our brains release in spades when we dance or reach a runner's high. Endorphins (like opioids) mask pain.

In some cases (but not all), people with CIP are successfully treated with naloxone, which is, coincidentally, a drug used in some hospitals and treatment centers to counter the effects of opioids. The staff doctor might prescribe naloxone to opioid-dependent patients during treatment to block opioid receptors, reduce cravings, and, in emergency situations, prevent overdose.

Other than having to endure pain or determine how to treat it safely, one of the more frustrating aspects of pain is how to measure it. Everyone, it seems, has a different pain threshold, or the upper limit of pain tolerance. Physicians can pull out the card with the ten different faces, each one progressively looking more uncomfortable, but a 5 for one individual might be an 8 for another individual suffering the same injury. Pain is not only physiological but also cultural. Some cultures teach people to endure pain while people in other cultures want instantaneous pain relief. For some people, pain may almost be a pleasurable confirmation that they are alive and well, and in others the discomfort is absolutely intolerable and needs to be relieved. This is also true for pain threshold sensitivity. What one person perceives as hot, another person perceives as extremely hot. What one person perceives as a 10 on the pain scale, another person perceives as a 4. We do get desensitized with pain when we experience it on a chronic basis.

What Is Chronic Pain?

Chronic pain is pain that is experienced regularly over a long duration; it is pain that continues beyond what would be considered a "normal healing process." What's considered a normal healing process varies, depending in part on what you're healing from, how old you are, how healthy you are physically, how healthy your attitude is, and how compliant you are with doctor's orders. Chronic pain can be linked to either injury or disease. When opioids are taken for extended periods to relieve chronic pain, chronic pain becomes the disease itself, resulting in opioid-induced hyperalgesia.

Treating Acute Pain: When and How to Use Opioid Painkillers Safely

Opioid painkillers probably aren't going away any time soon. Can we use them safely? Should we turn down these medications at the hospital or dentist? Should we discourage our parents from starting on a regimen of painkillers?

As a doctor in recovery, I don't advocate for pain over abstinence. For acute pain, whether your loved one has the disease of addiction or not, I advocate for safe, highly monitored use of painkillers in the right circumstances, in the proper doses, and with complete transparency. In other words, proceed with caution.

If your loved one is not addicted to alcohol or other drugs, know and understand that opioids are highly addictive substances.

For some people, they create an irresistible euphoria that begs repeating. Mom doesn't need to suffer, but if the prescription says to take "as needed," at some point, if you believe Mom can get by with half of the prescribed dose or with a non-addictive painkiller such as acetaminophen or ibuprofen, opt for the safer route. Mom can always take the opioid medication if she really needs it.

If Mom starts taking more than prescribed or if you believe she wants pills even when her condition is not causing pain, you are wise to start a conversation. Tell your family members, caregivers, her doctors, an addiction counselor, and anyone who will listen before it gets out of hand. Be transparent.

Opioids are powerful. Recovery rates, although improving, are not entirely promising. If the older adult you care for has the disease of addiction, following my words of caution is not optional but required. More than one person in recovery has relapsed after being prescribed morphine post-surgery and milder painkillers to take at home. This said, you need to know that many people in recovery, myself included, have successfully undergone multiple surgeries, received morphine drops afterward, taken painkillers as needed, and stayed loyal to themselves and the program. The difference between those who relapse and those who don't boils down to how transparent we are with ourselves, our physician, our family and friends, and, if we're in recovery, our Twelve Step community. When we're honest, we're not hiding anything about how we feel or how many pills we've taken.

The economics of pain management are about supply and demand. For someone in active addiction, or whose cravings have been stimulated, the demand will always increase and never go away. You need a system that removes the possibility of secretly taking extra medication, mixing medications, or visiting new doctors in search of prescriptions. So supply has to be limited. All patients need to have their pain medications rationed on a daily basis. Someone else needs to control the medication and not leave it out on the kitchen counter all day. If you live far away from your loved one, monitoring is best done at first in an extended care nursing facility. When it's time for discharge, nursing staff can transfer the responsibility to family members or home caregivers. The patient's medications can be set out on a daily basis. The patient is given a mechanism to request more pain medication should they need it. All medications must be transparent and accounted for. Now, no one needs to be a professional monitor to do this, but it is not the family's job to be in that position with an addict. You can hire professional pain medication monitors for addicts who report to the family. Monitoring is usually done with body fluid testing.

Treating Chronic Pain Safely

At the Betty Ford Center, we have a specialized track for patients who come into treatment addicted to painkillers and suffering from chronic pain. Most of the time, these patients have been taking painkillers for years and are sometimes completely unaware that their condition might be the result of taking the medication that is supposed to be helping them.

In many ways chronic pain parallels addiction, and so the biological, psychological, social, and spiritual model of addiction fits for chronic pain as well. There is usually shame associated with both. There is often unresolved trauma associated with both. So treating pain during treatment for substance misuse is natural.

At the Betty Ford Center, we first wean patients from their medication using a medically assisted detoxification process that manages withdrawal symptoms. We put them on safer medications so they are comfortable before they enter the pain program. One of the magical parts about the pain program is that people who become pain-medication-free are usually able to function better than they ever have. After the first day or so, the magic of hope enters the new patient's life. As patients start to get relief from their opium-induced hyperalgesia, the unbearable pain does not return. Much to their surprise their pain is decreased. Once they see a lot of their pain was fear and anxiety based—the anticipation of pain that may never come—this, too, produces hope for them. All pain is real from my perspective: psychological pain, traumatic pain, physical pain, noxious stimuli pain. Pain is real for the person who perceives it, and this must be validated. What we do about it and how we treat it may differ. Patients need to know that their pain is real and not just "in their head."

There may also be some significant pain during withdrawal. Patients on opioids usually feel like they are going to die. Many of them have had that experience on a smaller basis when they ran out of medications and were unable to contact their doctor. They went into panic mode. The thought of not having their drug during detox is a frightening experience until they realize that help is present. Then their fear and anxiety subside. Intense one-on-one therapy and the healing support of group therapies seem to bring relief to the great majority of patients.

Following is a list of some alternative therapies for drug-free pain management. They have all been proven to work, some better than others according to the patient's receptivity and degree of compliance. We use them in our pain management clinic at the Betty Ford Center every day with great success. Look into them, research them, find classes nearby, and, after consulting with an appropriate health care provider, help the older adult use them.

- acupuncture
- aromatherapy
- biofeedback

- chiropractic
- hypnotherapy
- massage
- relaxation therapy
- Tai Chi
- meditation
- mindfulness
- nutritional counseling, particularly to avoid inflammatory foods

There is some hope on the horizon for a non-mood-altering substance that helps to manage pain. Researchers continue to focus on developing medicine that kills pain but is less addictive.

A Note on Pain Management Clinics

Earlier in this book, I mentioned that I am not a fan of traditional pain management clinics, those that I call "pill mills." If your loved one is going to a pain management clinic, you would be wise to look into the clinic's process. A good pain management clinic will rely on alternative therapies more than drugs and will monitor patients for addiction. Anything short of that is unethical, in my opinion.

■

Epilogue

We've covered a lot of material in this book. If it helps you or an older adult in your life even marginally, I've done my job. If it changes lives for the better, you and your loved one have done your jobs.

You've got your marching orders. Your mission is to carry out the sacred work of taking care of your elder loved ones, to ensure they do not isolate, to make sure their quality of care is second to none. It's noble work.

Supporting you and your loved one or patient in pursuing a life free of mood-altering and unnecessary drugs is the goal of this book. But, in truth, that is only the beginning of the journey. For if we were unhappy and discontented before we started using drugs, we will likely be unhappy and discontented afterward. And the real goal should be about more than being drug-free.

The real journey is a spiritual one, and that is why the Twelve Step program has been so successful for millions of people from all walks of life. Working the Steps and being involved in the support groups give members a practical path to finding a relationship with a power greater than themselves—or as it's also known in the program, a "higher power" or the "God of your understanding." Whether older adults are religious or agnostic, they can discover—or rediscover—the greater meaning and purpose in their lives that comes with escaping the loneliness of being trapped in their own pain and egos. They can experience the magic of community, service, and the spiritual awakening promised in Step Twelve.

I invite you to read the essay "Spiritual Life Must Come First" by my good friend and colleague, the Reverend Charles Harper, that's included at the end of this book. He makes me feel that God and a spiritual life are accessible to a mere mortal like me.

When boiled down, spirituality is a change in perception, and it is essential to a happy and joyous and free recovery. It's never too late to begin this journey. In fact, in many ways, the last chapter in life can be our greatest motivator.

■

Spiritual Life Must Come First

by the Reverend Charles F. Harper

> The balance and peace we seek for ourselves and our society won't be achieved through mental effort alone. Mind and spirit are meant to travel together, with spirit leading the way. Until we make a conscious commitment to understand and embrace our spiritual nature, we will endure the ache of living without the awareness and guidance of the most essential part of ourselves.[43]
>
> —SUSAN L. TAYLOR

When we are down so low, everything looks up to us. If we look around we can see that to which we cling is usually the ephemeral, the temporary, that which has nothing to do with animating the internal part of ourselves: the spirit.

Certainly, ego wants us to hold on tight to that which is familiar, to that at which we feel competent, to that which is tangible, and all that is provable with facts. But those of us who believe in spirit know that our reality is latent with unseen existences. We also believe that the spirit itself is eternal. Yet we are far more likely to take our bodies for a walk than we are to exercise the soul.

The spirit is eternal, so wouldn't it then seem logical that's exactly the part that we should care for the most? The part that we should nurture and feed on a daily basis? The part of ourselves that we should learn the most about? Many of us learn about our body: what to feed it and how to exercise it and what it needs to help us feel better. Some of us even obsess about it. But as for our spirits, we do little.

We may go to church or synagogue or mosque once a week, we may even occasionally pray, listen to a good sermon, or surround ourselves with people who seem to be good or at least seem to be more acceptable to God. But our spirit is still a huge part of us—a part of us that is just waiting for us to pay attention to it—for it has many wonderful things that it will allow us to see and feel and experience if we just give it some attention!

How Do We Pay Attention to Spirit?

Pay attention to that which appears "greater" than self. At the risk of being enigmatic, in time it will be revealed to you that there is something greater than "self" out there. If you are open to miracles, it cannot be helped. You see, a miracle is simply a shift in perception. And how can our perception of our place in the universe not shift as our mindfulness and awareness of our "selves" in the family of beings expands? This mindfulness can take place in the quietude of aloneness or at the foot of a giant sequoia, in words of poetry or theater that transform the human spirit, or in music that lifts and holds our emotions like memories and dreams or on a mountain trembling with hugeness.

Nevertheless you may ask yourself, what is it that I don't believe in? The god that is rejected by the atheist or agnostic is usually the god that does not exist, namely the god who delivers us the winning lottery ticket and saves us from fire-breathing drones.

On the contrary, for me God has protected me from nothing. But so far God has sustained me in everything. God then is not some being or energy up there playing celestial checkers with my life, rather it is my faith. My faith is simply an awareness of my life flowing from and sustained by a force outside of my "self." And at its best, my spirit emanating from the seat of my soul is in concert with that force.

"I am who I am." God therefore is being. God is source. The source of our authentic being. God is that holy part of self that is not subject even to the brutality of my wreckage and self-will run riot.

God is alpha and omega. And what is it that never ends? Love. This force cannot be described by me as anything other than love, or agape. To believe that anything other than love can define me is idolatry. In this way, no matter what the outcome of my choices, or the "slings and arrows of outrageous fortune," there is always the possibility of infinite love to be found in the outcome. God is simply a word that is used to express the infinity of the moment I am in right now.

If I believe my origin is God, then of course, I am God's gift to the world. If God's life pulses through me, then when I deny it, I die. Now I am not saying I am God, nor am I other than God. Simply what happens to me or my brothers and sisters happens to God. What happens to God happens to me.

So the first step in our spirituality is to surrender. We may not surrender our intent, nor will we surrender our actions, but we do surrender all expectations of outcomes. We don't just surrender but, as Kierkegaard put it, we come to a place of "infinite resignation,"[44] when we release all of our illusory control of personal ambitions, self-will, and projected optimistic outcomes. And what is it we surrender to? We surrender to truth. And what is the truth? Love is the truth. And if love is the truth, then love must be God because God is truth. So when I turn my life and will over to love I surrender to the love that is God. Anne Morrow Lindbergh said "Love is a force . . . It is not a result; it is a cause. It is not a product; it produces. It is a power, like money, or steam or electricity. It is valueless unless you can give something else *by means* of it."[45]

When we surrender to love, when we use it as a force to shape our reality or at least our perceptions of reality, then our anger, fear, hurt, guilt, and shame can be transfigured by the power of love itself into serenity, faith, joy, forgiveness, and humility.

This belief can lead us to a mystical life, which is our ability and willingness to recognize the holiness in all people, the immense loveliness of even the least of us, the rise of the sun, and the blossom of flowers. True mysticism is to look "not at what I've done; rather look what God's love has done for me."

Pay attention to your religious heritage, if you have one at all. At its best, religion through its liturgy and music and sermons and prayers empowers us to encounter the universal mystery of spiritual awakening. Having said that, religions are a collective ego; as such they have thrived and survived on a tribal consciousness, which has done much to divide the human race. One only has to look at religion-inspired events in the Middle East to see that this world cannot survive religion based on tribal consciousness.

Whether we call our "selves" religious or spiritual, all of us are called to discipleship. Discipleship is simply intimacy with the infinite facilitated by solitude, aloneness, music, nature, prayer, meditation, and so on.

In my discipleship, whether I'm guided by the principles of spirituality or the creed and dogma of organized religion, my litmus test for what is useful to me on "the road less traveled" is best described by Allen Ginsberg when he wrote, "Well, while I'm here I'll do the work —And what's the work? To ease the pain of living. Everything else, drunken dumbshow."[46]

Pay attention to anger, fear, hurt, guilt, and shame. When we are not paying attention to the spirit—the spirit that blows where it will and where it goes nobody knows—we find ourselves in a place of anger, fear, hurt, guilt for things we have done wrong and have left undone, and shame, a false belief that we are not enough. Each of these pushes us into a place of such dissonance between who we are authentically and the false persona we project that discomfort leads us to all forms of self-medication.

The root of all anger is the belief that we should be somewhere other than where we stand in the present. For example, if your level of irritation and frustration rises when standing at the end of the line in a grocery store, it is because you believe you should be someplace other than at the end of the line in a grocery store. In reality you are exactly where you should be. When we come to a place where we truly accept that we are where we are supposed to be, the inevitable outcome is "the peace that passes all understanding," namely serenity.

Fear, or as they say in my fellowship, "false evidence appearing real," is based on the ego's belief that there is not enough, that there will never be enough, and that tomorrow will not take care of itself. It is a denial that today well lived makes every yesterday a fond memory and every tomorrow a day of hope. But when we surrender to love, that which we fear becomes shaped by gratitude—gratitude for what we received in the past and for what we have in the moment. For example, I have a great deal of faith in retrospect. I can look back on my life and, no matter what tragedies and cruelties and traumas may have beset me, I seem to have survived and in some cases thrived. Yet when it comes to faith and prospect, or what is in the future, I can readily devolve into a place of fear—fear that is as real as believing that nothing good could come of this event. But when I'm in a place of gratitude for what

I have, where I am, the gifts, talents, the nascent virtues I have begun to manifest, my gratitude leads me to faith, a faith that at times allows me to take premeditated leaps into the darkness and to accept change as a gift. And growth is the fruit of change.

The next thing we must become aware of is hurt. The pain and suffering that is universal to the human experience is unique to each and every one of us. Sometimes despite our best intentions and despite our spiritual progress, we wake up with an overwhelming feeling that we can't go on. We might call it depression. We might call it self-pity. We might call it anxiety. Just because we are on a spiritual path does not mean that we wake up every morning singing: "Yes, this is the day the Lord has made, I will rejoice and be glad in it!" If you feel depressed, if you feel anxious, if you feel self-pity then allow yourself to feel it. What's the problem? When you dive deep into the heart of that which is causing you angst, you may discover the most spiritual feeling of all—a much misunderstood gateway to grace as sacred as the most profound joy.

In consciousness, the difference is that we go into our pain knowingly. We touch it over and over again with the love that is in us and around us. This time when we are feeling angst we abandon the drama, the justifications, the blaming, and we just embrace the raw and broken heart, a fresh wound reopened in love with no desire to escape it at all. In this place you forge a new spirituality with your courage. We infuse the sadness with our light, with our understanding, with our willingness and openness to see the divine in everything, everywhere. Believe me, this could save us: Be courageous enough to feel our aches and pains consciously without numbing ourselves or turning away from the pain.

Allowing ourselves to be aware of everything from the aches

and pains of our life to cruelties, tragedies, and traumas, allowing ourselves to wade through the phenomenon of grief even when it leads to periods of depression or sends us back on a path of tears, allows us to experience and become aware of the joys of life. In our addiction we attempted to assuage our hurt and pain and sorrows with our drug of choice. And in so doing we could never experience true joy or true happiness. But by inviting our hurt and our pain to tea and learning what it has to teach us, we open the door to that which gives us pleasure and joy.

Guilt is what we have done and what we have left undone. Some call it the wreckage of life. It is here where we enlist the power of compassion, for ourselves and for others. For most of us, compassion can transform guilt into forgiveness. We can find it difficult to have compassion for ourselves, even when we can exercise extreme empathy for others. Compassion becomes most difficult for those who have done us personal harm. But it is here that we are called to compassion that is 7 × 70 in its power. For those who have crossed us or hurt us consciously or unconsciously, our compassion is even greater because we know they are following a road to personal perdition. As for forgiving ourselves, remember that you are not the same person you were ten years ago, five years ago, or even a year ago! What right have you to condemn the young man who made mistakes and perhaps even learned from them? What right do you have to not forgive the young boy who could not defend himself against emotional or physical or sexual abuse? If we are on a path of personal growth and self-actualization, our value, resources, and perspectives will shift with time and will demand forgiveness of self for all that was left undone and all that was done.

Martin Luther once said "Sin boldly!," by which he meant all of us imperfect members of the human race in our intent, action, or outcome will create some offense. In this way Luther believed we are all in need of forgiveness, and we are all in need to forgive.

We must be aware of our shame, as in "we are not enough." To live in a place of shame is to be dishonest with yourself. It is to lie to yourself about who you really are. Shame, you see, tells us that we are not enough. But how could we not be enough if we are children of God? So to move from shame to humility, we must embrace honesty.

In an essay on lies and secrets from *Divergent*, the author speaks of her vision for an honest world.

> In this world, parents do not lie to their children, and children do not lie to their parents; friends do not lie to one another; spouses do not lie to each other. When we are asked our opinions we are free to give them without having to consider any other responses. When we engage in conversation with others, we do not have to evaluate their intentions, because they are transparent. We have no suspicion, and no one suspects us. And most of all—yes, above all else—we are free to expose our dark secrets because we know the dark secrets of our neighbors, our friends, our spouses, our children, our parents, and our enemies. We know that while we are flawed in a unique way, we are not unique because we are flawed. Therefore we can be authentic. We have no suspicions. And we are at peace with those around us.[47]

We all have a shadow side, or what St. Francis of Assisi called an "inner leper." We also have what Abraham Lincoln, in his First Inaugural Address, called "the better Angels of our nature." When we are in a place of shame we only see our inner leper and ignore the better Angels of our nature. When we are honest we embrace our inner leper, and we feed the better Angels of our nature; we come to a place of humility where we recognize and celebrate our perfection in imperfection as people.

You do know it will require a certain fortitude of spirit, including the courage to find intimacy by never running away from aloneness—coming out from behind a stand of trees and laying yourself open to vulnerability. On a granite rock you will sit asking the rock where it has been and where it is going, and you will know solitude: a time where you will be expected to be present to the inexpressible. You will know times of sustained pondering. Of course, you will find yourself abandoning all that is less than the infinite, all those props of image and status that are used for security and identity. And we will grieve. Our grieving is simply our willingness to leave behind so that we might enter where we've never been before.

It is here—in "the winter of our discontent" or "our dark night of the soul"—that we wean ourselves from all finite means of depending on the shifting resources of that which is seen . . . so that we might go into the desert of our nothingness and in that desert encounter the Divine.

Rev. Charles F. Harper
September 2015
Author of *Amazing Grief! A Healing Guide for Parents of Young Addicts*
Co-Founder/Spiritual Director, Whole Soul Recovery Community,
Faith Counseling for Teens and Families in Crisis

"Spiritual Life Must Come First" is included with permission from Charles F. Harper.

Resources

For Alcoholics and Addicts

Alcoholics Anonymous World Services, aa.org

Narcotics Anonymous World Services, na.org

Hazelden Betty Ford Foundation, hazeldenbettyford.org, 24-hour helpline: 1-866-831-5700

AARP, aarp.org

Alcoholics Anonymous, fourth edition. New York: Alcoholics Anonymous World Services, Inc., 2001

Conquer Chronic Pain: An Innovative Mind-Body Approach, by Peter Przekop, DO, PhD. Center City, MN: Hazelden Publishing, 2015

Each Day a New Beginning: Daily Meditations for Women, by Karen Casey. Center City, MN: Hazelden Publishing, 1982

Finding a Home Group, by James G. Center City, MN: Hazelden Publishing, 2011

Getting Started in AA, by Hamilton B. Center City, MN: Hazelden Publishing, 1995

Narcotics Anonymous, sixth edition. Van Nuys, CA: Narcotics Anonymous World Services, Inc., 2008

Twenty-Four Hours a Day. Center City, MN: Hazelden Publishing, 1975

Undrunk: A Skeptic's Guide to AA, by A. J. Adams. Center City, MN: Hazelden Publishing, 2009

A Woman's Way through the Twelve Steps, by Stephanie Covington. Center City, MN: Hazelden Publishing, 1994

For Families

Al-Anon Family Groups, al-anon.alateen.org

Nar-Anon Family Groups, nar-anon.org

Co-Dependents Anonymous World Fellowship (CoDA), coda.org

AARP, aarp.org

Substance Abuse and Mental Health Services Administration (SAMHSA) treatment finder, samhsa.gov/treatment

Addict in the Family: Stories of Loss, Hope, and Recovery, Revised and Updated, by Beverly Conyers. Center City, MN: Hazelden Publishing, 2015

Codependent No More: How to Stop Controlling Others and Start Caring for Yourself, by Melody Beattie. Center City, MN: Hazelden Publishing, 1986

Detachment and Enabling, by Rebecca D. Chaitin and Judith M. Knowlton. Center City, MN: Hazelden Publishing, 1985

Everything Changes: Help for Families of Newly Recovering Addicts, by Beverly Conyers. Center City, MN: Hazelden Publishing, 2009

How Al-Anon Works for Families and Friends of Alcoholics. Virginia Beach, VA: Al-Anon Family Group Headquarters, Inc., 1995

Language of Letting Go, by Melody Beattie. Center City, MN: Hazelden Publishing, 1990

Love First: A Family's Guide to Intervention, second edition, by Jeff Jay and Debra Jay. Center City, MN: Hazelden Publishing, 2008

Now What: An Insider's Guide to Addiction and Recovery, by William Cope Moyers. Center City, MN: Hazelden Publishing, 2012

Notes

1. Betty Ford, *Betty: A Glad Awakening* (New York: Doubleday, 1987), 7.

2. Center for Substance Abuse Treatment, *Substance Abuse Among Older Adults*, Treatment Improvement Protocol (TIP) Series, no. 26, (Rockville, MD: Substance Abuse and Mental Health Services Administration, 1998), 1.

3. Beth Han, Joseph C. Gfroerer, James D. Colliver, and Michael A. Penne, "Substance Use Disorder among Older Adults in the United States in 2020," *Addiction* 104 (2009): 88–96, www.ncbi.nlm.nih.gov/pubmed/19133892.

4. National Council on Alcoholism and Drug Dependence, "Alcohol, Drug Dependence and Seniors," last modified June 26, 2015, www.ncadd.org/about-addiction/seniors/alcohol-drug-dependence-and-seniors.

5. Kevin Pollard and Paola Scommegna, "Just How Many Baby Boomers Are There?," Population Reference Bureau, April 2014, www.prb.org/Publications/Articles/2002/JustHowManyBabyBoomersAreThere.aspx; and Pew Research Center, "Baby Boomers Retire," December 29, 2010, www.pewresearch.org/daily-number/baby-boomers-retire/.

6. Celia Vimont, "Baby Boomers Continue Substance Use as They Age," Partnership for Drug-Free Kids, October 22, 2013, www.drugfree.org/join-together/baby-boomers-continue-substance-use-as-they-age/.

7. Substance Abuse and Mental Health Services Administration, *Results from the 2011 National Survey on Drug Use and Health: Summary of National Findings*, NSDUH Series H-44, HHS Publication No. (SMA) 12-4713 (Rockville, MD: Substance Abuse and Mental Health Services Administration, 2012).

8. Janet Loehrke and Peter Eisler, "Seniors and Prescription Drugs: As Misuse Rises, So Does the Toll," *USA Today*, May 22, 2014, www.usatoday.com/story/news/nation/2014/05/20/seniors-addiction-prescription-drugs-painkillers/9277489/.

9. Walter Ling, Larissa Mooney, and Maureen Hillhouse, "Prescription Opioid Abuse, Pain and Addiction: Clinical Issues and Implications," *Drug Alcohol Review* 30, no. 3 (May 2011): 300–305, www.ncbi.nlm.nih.gov/pubmed/21545561.

10. U.S. Census Bureau, *65+ in the United States: 2010*, (Washington, DC: U.S. Government Printing Office, 2014), 36, www.census.gov/content/dam/Census/library/publications/2014/demo/p23-212.pdf.

11. University of Pennsylvania Health System, "Stairway to Recovery," 2003, www.uphs.upenn.edu/addiction/berman/family/addiction.html.

12. The Henry J. Kaiser Family Foundation, "Total Number of Retail Prescription Drugs Filled at Pharmacies," http://kff.org/other/state-indicator/total-retail-rx-drugs/; Marie N. Stagnitti, *Statistical Brief #168: Trends in Outpatient Prescription Drug Utilization and Expenditures, 1997 and 2004* (Rockville, MD: Agency for Healthcare Research and Quality, 2007), 1, http://meps.ahrq.gov/mepsweb/data_files/publications/st168/stat168.pdf.

13. Michael Walsh (president and CEO, National Association of Addiction Treatment Providers), in discussion with the author, February 19, 2015.

14. William Strauss and Neil Howe, *Generations: The History of America's Future, 1584 to 2069* (New York: Harper Perennial, 1991), 52.

15. David W. Kaufman, Judith P. Kelly, Lynn Rosenberg, Theresa E. Anderson, and Allen A. Mitchell. "Recent Patterns of Medication Use in the Ambulatory Adult Population of the United States: The Slone Survey," *Journal of the American Medical Association* 287, no. 3 (2002): 337–44.

16. National Institute on Alcohol Abuse and Alcoholism, "Alcohol Alert (No. 27 PH 355)," January 1995, last updated October 2000, http://pubs.niaaa.nih.gov/publications/aa27.htm.

17. Robert L. Maher Jr., Joseph T. Hanlon, and Emily R. Hajjar, "Clinical Consequences of Polypharmacy in Elderly," *Expert Opinion on Drug Safety* 13, no. 1 (2014): 57–65, http://tandfonline.com/doi/full/10.1517/14740338.2013.827660.

18. *Substance Abuse Among Older Adults*, 6.

19. U.S. Food and Drug Administration, "Strategies to Reduce Medication Errors: Working to Improve Medication Safety," last updated October 23, 2015, www.fda.gov/Drugs/ResourcesForYou/Consumers/ucm143553.htm.

20. World Health Organization, "10 Facts on Dementia," March 2015, www.who.int/features/factfiles/dementia/en/.

21. *2015 Alzheimer's Disease Facts and Figures*, Alzheimer's Association, 2015, 5, www.alz.org/facts/downloads/facts_figures_2015.pdf.

22. Kaufman et al., "Recent Patterns of Medication Use," 337–44.

23. Shih-Wei Lai, Chih-Hsueh Lin, Kuan-Fu Liao, Li-Ting Su, Fung-Chang Sung, and Cheng-Chieh Lin, "Association between Polypharmacy and Dementia in Older People: A Population-Based Case-Control Study in Taiwan," *Geriatrics & Gerontology International* 12, no. 3 (July 2012): 491–8, http://onlinelibrary.wiley.com/doi/10.1111/j.1447-0594.2011.00800.x/abstract.

24. David S. Knopman, Ronald C. Petersen, Ruth H. Cha, Steven D. Edland, and Walter A Rocca, "Incidence and Causes of Nondegenerative Nonvascular Dementia: A Population-Based Study," *Archives of Neurology* 63, no. 2 (2006): 218–221.

25. Pain Killer Abuse, "Prescription Drug Statistics," www.painkillerabuse.us/content/prescription-drug-statistics.html.

26. UnityPoint Health: Illinois Institute for Addiction Recovery, "Sedative/Hypnotics," www.addictionrecov.org/Addictions/?AID=38.

27. National Institute on Drug Abuse, "Overdose Death Rates," revised February 2015, www.drugabuse.gov/related-topics/trends-statistics/overdose-death-rates.

28. *Older Americans Behavioral Health, Issue Brief 5: Prescription Medication Misuse and Abuse Among Older Adults*, Substance Abuse and Mental Health Services Administration, 2012, www.aoa.acl.gov/AoA_Programs/HPW/Behavioral/docs2/Issue%20Brief%205%20Prescription%20Med%20Misuse%20Abuse.pdf.

29. The White House, "New Data Reveal 400% Increase in Substance Abuse Treatment Admissions for People Abusing Prescription Drugs," July 15, 2010, www.whitehouse.gov/ondcp/news-releases-remarks/new-data-reveal-increase-in-substance-abuse-treatment-admissions.

30. Loehrke and Eisler, "Seniors and Prescription Drugs: As Misuse Rises, So Does the Toll."

31. "In a Move by the U.S. Department of Health and Human Services—Patient Limit on Access to Opioid Dependence Treatments to Be Expanded," PRNewswire, September 18, 2015, www.prnewswire.com/news-releases/in-a-move-by-the-us-department-of-health-and-human-services--patient-limit-on-access-to-opioid-dependence-treatments-to-be-expanded-300145557.html.

32. Centers for Disease Control and Prevention, "Home and Recreational Safety: Important Facts about Falls," last updated September 21, 2015, www.cdc.gov/HomeandRecreationalSafety/Falls/adultfalls.html.

33. National Institute on Drug Abuse, "Drugs, Brains, and Behavior: The Science of Addiction," updated July 2014, www.drugabuse.gov/publications/science-addiction/drugs-brain.

34. Johanna O'Flaherty, *The Correlation between Trauma and Addiction* (Las Vegas: Central Recovery Press, 2014), Kindle edition, chapter 1.

35. U.S. Census Bureau, *65+ in the United States*, 36.

36. *Caregiving in the U.S. 2009*, National Alliance for Caregiving in Collaboration with AARP, November 2009, http://assets.aarp.org/rgcenter/il/caregiving_09_fr.pdf.

37. *Chronic Conditions: Making the Case for Ongoing Care*, Partnership for Solutions, September 2004, www.partnershipforsolutions.org/DMS/files/chronicbook2004.pdf.

38. Susan C. Reinhard, Carol Levine, and Sarah Samis, *Home Alone: Family Caregivers Providing Complex Chronic Care* (Washington DC: AARP, October 2012), www.aarp.org/content/dam/aarp/research/public_policy_institute/health/home-alone-family-caregivers-providing-complex-chronic-care-rev-AARP-ppi-health.pdf.

39. *The National Elder Abuse Incidence Study: Final Report*, National Center on Elder Abuse, September 1998, http://aoa.gov/AoA_Programs/Elder_Rights/Elder_Abuse/docs/ABuseReport_Full.pdf.

40. National Institute on Drug Abuse, "Drug Facts: Understanding Drug Abuse and Addiction," last updated November 2012, www.drugabuse.gov/publications/drugfacts/understanding-drug-abuse-addiction.

41. *Principles of Drug Addiction Treatment: A Research-Based Guide*, 3rd ed., National Institute on Drug Abuse, revised December 2012, https://d14rmgtrwzf5a.cloudfront.net/sites/default/files/podat_1.pdf.

42. *Pain Management Fact Sheet*, National Institutes of Health, updated October 2010, http://report.nih.gov/nihfactsheets/Pdfs/PainManagement(NINR).pdf.

43. Susan L. Taylor, *Lessons in Living* (New York: Anchor Books, 1998), 147.

44. Søren Kierkegaard, Alastair Hannay, transl., *Fear and Trembling* (New York: Penguin Books, 2003).

45. Larry Chang, editor and compiler, *Wisdom for the Soul: Five Millennia of Prescriptions for Spiritual Healing* (Washington DC: Gnosophia Publishers, 2006), 564.

46. Allen Ginsberg, "Memory Gardens," in *Collected Poems 1946–1997* (New York: HarperCollins, 2007), 539.

47. Veronica Roth, *Divergent* (New York: Katherine Tegen Books, 2011).

About the Author

As physician director of professional and residential programs at the Betty Ford Center—part of the Hazelden Betty Ford Foundation—in Rancho Mirage, California, for the past eight years, Harry L. Haroutunian, MD, has used his training and firsthand experience with addiction to successfully work with thousands of patients in treatment, ranging from high-profile celebrities and CEOs to stay-at-home moms and older adults. He is board certified in both addiction and family medicine, and is an internationally known speaker and authority on addiction-oriented topics. He has appeared on *The Dr. Oz Show* and *Dr. Drew on Call* and in the *New York Times* and *Cosmopolitan* magazine, and he is widely read online.

Prior to joining the newly merged Hazelden Betty Ford Foundation, Dr. Haroutunian (or "Dr. Harry, as he is affectionately known to his patients) practiced family and sports medicine in southern Vermont for more than thirty years. During this time, he developed a special place in his heart for older adults with addiction problems. A large percentage of Dr. Harry's clients were older adults, many of whom came into his office suffering from the effects of bad drug combinations, and some had become dependent on their medications. A member of the Council on Aging in Vermont, Dr. Harry worked closely with all its home programs and attended patients at elder-care facilities. In addition, Dr. Harry's three-generation household kept him active in the senior community. Much of his volunteer work revolved around connecting older adults with volunteer and social opportunities—everything from helping them to become teachers' aides in schools to joining bowling leagues. At the Betty Ford Center, Dr. Harry continues to see many older adults affected by the disease of addiction.

Dr. Harry is the author of *Being Sober: Getting to, Getting through, and Staying in Recovery* (Rodale, 2013), a Twelve Step–based trade paperback for people contemplating or in recovery from alcohol and other drug addiction, as well as for family members and other loved ones. Released in August 2013, *Being Sober* has only gained in popularity since it began circulating through the recovery community. He also created *Recovery 101*, a series of taped lectures on the topics of addiction medicine, recovery issues, communication skills, spirituality, and relapse prevention. This DVD series is used throughout the country by treatment facilities, family-care programs, and medical schools to educate new doctors. The thousands of patients admitted to the Hazelden Betty Ford Foundation, as well as those in the Family Program, hear a live lecture from Dr. Harry during their stay. Afterward, many patients head directly to the campus bookstore to purchase his book and DVD lecture series. After leaving treatment, some find inspiration by seeking him out in one of his nine YouTube videos.

Dr. Harry earned his medical degree from Albany Medical College of Union University in Albany, New York. He is a member of the American Academy of Family Physicians, California Academy of Family Physicians, American Society of Addiction Medicine, American Medical Association, American Board of Addiction Medicine, and American Board of Family Medicine. He is certified by the American Board of Family Physicians and American Board of Addiction Medicine. Since the release of *Being Sober*, Dr. Harry has served on the Substance Abuse Advisory Board for the Screen Actors Guild, on the Substance Abuse Advisory Board for the American Bar Association's Lawyer Assistance Programs, and on the Advisory Board for Alliance for a Healthier Generation, supported by the American Heart Association and the Clinton Foundation.

After thirty years in family medicine, Dr. Harry found himself suffering from alcohol addiction. Like Father Damien among the lepers, he had become one of the very people he was trying to help. He had the disease that killed his brother, his father, and two uncles. He had the disease that affected his son and nephew. He had the medical knowledge and, indeed, the arrogance of a physician hoping to think his way around this disease and who found over and over again it simply does not work. Finally, Dr. Harry became sober for good.

About Hazelden Publishing

As part of the Hazelden Betty Ford Foundation, Hazelden Publishing offers both cutting-edge educational resources and inspirational books. Our print and digital works help guide individuals in treatment and recovery, and their loved ones. Professionals who work to prevent and treat addiction also turn to Hazelden Publishing for evidence-based curricula, digital content solutions, and videos for use in schools, treatment programs, correctional programs, and electronic health records systems. We also offer training for implementation of our curricula.

Through published and digital works, Hazelden Publishing extends the reach of healing and hope to individuals, families, and communities affected by addiction and related issues.